CRANKS

CAKES & BISCUITS

Compiled by Daphne Swann

© Cranks Ltd and Guinness Publishing Ltd 1988
Recipe development Valerie Fisher
Editor Beatrice Frei
Art editor David Roberts
Illustrations Suzanne Alexander, Edward Bawden and Jane Lydbury
Photographs Grant Symon, food prepared by Jane Suthering
Pottery for photography kindly loaned by Craftsmen Potters Shop, Marshall
Street, London W1.
Published in Great Britain by Guinness Publishing Ltd,
33 London Road, Enfield, Middlesex, England.

British Library Cataloguing in Publication Data
Cranks, Ltd.
    Cranks cakes and biscuits.
    1. Cakes using natural food – Recipes
    I. Title
    641.8'653

ISBN 0-85112-886-6

Typeset by Ace Filmsetting Ltd, Frome, Somerset
Printed and bound in Spain by Graficas Reunidas S.A., Madrid

INTRODUCTION

When Cranks opened its first restaurant 27 years ago (in Carnaby Street in London's Soho) its name exactly reflected how most people viewed wholefood and vegetarian restaurants – nutty in more senses than one! Now, of course, the lonely furrow that Cranks then ploughed has become the broad highway for a great many.

From the very beginning Cranks became something of a cult and throughout has remained the benchmark by which all other similar enterprises have to be judged. Not only has there been an unswerving commitment to wholefood and vegetarian food without additives and preservatives (to this day Cranks still uses flours from Pimhill Farm in Shropshire, which was one of the first to become totally organic) but there has also been a vigorous experimentation, innovation and creation of new dishes. And although now the food served at any of Cranks' expanding family of restaurants is sophisticated by comparison with the relatively simple fare of the earliest days, there still remains a satisfying practicality and unfussiness in the recipes which is a refreshing change from the pretentiousness of many restaurants and cookbooks.

The continual creation of new dishes has, over the years, produced a vast number of tried and tested recipes – and it's from this repertoire of new dishes that the very best have been selected for inclusion in this series of books.

NOTES ON INGREDIENTS

Agar The vegetarian substitute for gelatine. It is derived from a sea vegetable and produces a slightly cloudy jelly when set. It is available as a powder or in flakes.

Apple concentrate This syrupy brown concentrated apple juice is available in bottles in most health food shops.

Butter Cranks recommends using an unsalted butter. Vegetarian margarine may, of course, be substituted in all recipes where butter is stated.

Carob The ideal substitute for chocolate. It is made from the ground fruit of the carob tree. Available ground in powder form, in chips, drops or as a bar which can be grated, melted down or simply eaten like chocolate. It is rich in vitamins, contains no refined sugar or caffeine. Available in most health food shops.

Citrus Fruits Thoroughly wash all citrus rinds before using to remove any chemical deposits. Better still, use organically grown fruit.

Coconut Can be bought in various forms – desiccated or shredded (which is finely grated and dried) or creamed. The latter is sold in bars or tubs and can be broken off and melted for use in cooking. Coconut milk powder is sold like dried milk. All can be found in good health food stores or oriental shops.

Coffee Decaffeinated coffee either beans, ground, or instant is now readily available. Look out for the water extraction method which is generally recognized as being a better way of decaffeinating.

Couscous A semolina made from hardwheat moistened and rolled in flour. It is used extensively in the Middle East as a grain to accompany spicy stews.

Sold ready to cook in health food shops. Follow directions on the packet.

Eggs Cranks uses only free-range eggs in its bakeries and therefore recommends their use in all recipes. Many free-range eggs are not graded but as a guideline we would use size 3. They are now readily available in most shops – do be sure to look for the label "free-range".

Flour Cranks uses 100 per cent wholemeal stoneground and organically grown flour in all recipes – thus using the whole of the wheat berry. White flour has all the valuable bran and germ removed.

Freezing Recipes which are suitable for freezing will be marked by asterisks ***.

Lebnie A very low fat, stiff and concentrated Loseley product made from yoghourt. Obtainable from good healthfood shops. Quark would make an acceptable alternative.

Oil Sunflower, safflower and soya oil are all good to use in cooking, being mild in flavour and low in saturated fats.

Sugar Unrefined brown sugar is used in all Cranks recipes. It is free from artificial colourings and other additives and is available in six types – Demerara, light muscovado, muscovado, molasses, golden granulated and caster. For authenticity check the pack for the country of origin, usually Mauritius.

Tahini A thick oily paste made from roasted sesame seeds and rich in fat, protein and minerals – may be thinned down with water.

Toasting Nuts and Seeds Large nuts such as peanuts, hazelnuts, almonds, walnuts, as well as desiccated coconut and cereal flakes may be dry roasted in the oven at 350°F/180°C/gas mark 4 until golden brown. Seeds are better toasted in a dry pan on the stove, stirring frequently to prevent burning.

CAKES & BISCUITS

Cakes and biscuits have a special place in our diet, often forming the centre-piece for a party or special celebration. Though they may be considered an unnecessary luxury, they are nevertheless a most pleasurable indulgence and particularly when prepared with wholesome ingredients, they are both nutritious and sustaining.

In this book a whole series of new recipes has been introduced to add to our already well-tried repertoire and many of them, prepared in our bakery, will be found in our shops and restaurants. There are a number of sugarless or dairy-free recipes like the unusual Strawberry Couscous Cake, Malt & Apple Loaf and Fruity Nut Bars which are popular with children and such favourites as Gingerbread Men and a romantic Valentine Biscuit. There is the Cranks version of a Battenburg cake, which is fun and challenging to make, some deliciously rich and exciting gâteaux, cheesecakes and sponges and a number of mouthwatering biscuits like Coffee & Walnut Fingers which literally melt in the mouth! We have used only 100 per cent wholewheat, organically grown flour in all these recipes, unrefined brown sugar, honey, maple syrup or natural fruit juices for sweetening and always free-range eggs.

At the end of the book are a number of recipes for pastry making, cake decorations, fillings, icings and pastes. Most of the cakes and biscuits are best eaten fresh, especially those made with choux or puff pastry. Most of them are suitable for freezing and this will be indicated at the foot of the recipe by three asterisks ***. A number of recipes are suitable for those on a vegan diet or can readily be adapted to suit vegans such as substituting soya milk for milk, and margarine for butter.

WHOLEMEAL WHISKED SPONGE

This is a basic recipe, light and delicious with jam, or used as a basis for any number of more elaborate cakes and gâteaux.

Free-range eggs 4
Unrefined brown sugar 5 oz (150 g)
Vanilla essence ½ tsp (2.5 ml)
Wholemeal flour 3 oz (75 g)
Soya flour 1 oz (25 g)
Sugar-free raspberry or strawberry jam to fill
Whipped cream, optional

Whisk the eggs and sugar over a saucepan of simmering water, until very pale, thick and creamy. Remove from the heat, whisk in the vanilla essence, then fold in the wholemeal flour and soya flour. Transfer to two buttered and base-lined 8 in (20 cm) sandwich tins. Bake for about 20 minutes at 350°F/ 180°C/gas mark 4 until pale, golden and springy to the touch.

Cool on a wire tray, then fill with jam or fruit and whipped cream.

Variations
Carob
Replace 1 oz/25 g of the flour with carob powder.

Coffee
Add 2 tsp/10 ml of instant coffee powder to the flour.

Orange or Lemon
Replace the vanilla essence with finely grated rind of 1 orange or lemon.
***

WHOLEMEAL SPONGE FINGERS

Free-range eggs 3
Unrefined brown sugar 3 oz (75 g)
Vanilla essence ¼ tsp (1.25 ml)
Wholemeal flour 4 oz (100 g)

Place the eggs, sugar and vanilla essence in a bowl over a saucepan of simmering water and whisk until very thick and pale (the whisk should leave a strong trail in the mixture). Remove from the heat and carefully fold in the flour. Spoon the mixture into a piping bag fitted with a ½ in (1.5 cm) plain nozzle and pipe finger lengths about 4 in (10 cm) of sponge mixture on to buttered baking trays, allowing room for spreading. Bake at 375°F/190°C/gas mark 5 for 5–7 minutes until just firm to the touch. Cool on a wire tray.

Variations
Lemon
Omit the vanilla essence and add finely grated rind of 1 lemon.

Orange
Omit the vanilla essence and add finely grated rind of 1 orange.

Almond
Replace 1 oz/25 g flour with ground almonds and substitute almond essence for the vanilla essence.

Carob
Replace 1 tbsp/15 ml of the flour with carob powder.

Makes 30–35
***

CREAM SPONGE FINGERS

Sandwich wholemeal sponge fingers together with
whipped cream or thick set yoghourt with jam or
Cranks Raw Sugar Lemon Curd (see p. 86).

ALL-IN-ONE WHOLEMEAL SANDWICH CAKE

A quick and easy adaptation of the classic recipe for
today's soft polyunsaturated margarines.

Soft margarine 4 oz (100 g)
Unrefined brown sugar 4 oz (100 g)
Free-range eggs 3
Water 1 tbsp (15 ml)
Vanilla essence ½ tsp (2.5 ml)
Self-raising wholemeal flour 4 oz (100 g)
Baking powder 1 tsp (5 ml)
Raw sugar jam 4–6 tbsp (60–90 ml)
Ground almonds to decorate

Place the margarine, sugar, eggs, water, vanilla
essence, flour and baking powder in a bowl or food
processor. Beat until very light and fluffy. Divide the
mixture between two oiled and base-lined 7 in
(18 cm) sandwich tins. Level the surface. Bake at
350°F/180°C/gas mark 4 for 20–25 minutes or until
golden and springy to the touch. Cool on a wire tray.
Sandwich together with jam and use a sieve to
sprinkle ground almonds evenly over the surface.

Variation
For a special occasion, replace the vanilla essence with
finely grated rind of 1 lemon and sandwich with
lemon curd folded into whipped double cream.
***

HONEY, LEMON & GINGER SQUARES

Butter 6 oz (175 g)
Honey 3 oz (75 g)
Lemon, finely grated rind of 1
Self-raising wholemeal flour 6 oz (175 g)
Ground ginger ¾ tsp (3.75 ml)
Crystallized ginger, chopped 1½ oz (40 g)
Free-range eggs, beaten 2

TOPPING
Honey 1 tbsp (15 ml)
Lemon, juice of 1

Melt the butter and honey together in a saucepan and add the grated lemon rind. Remove from the heat and cool slightly. Add the remaining ingredients and mix well with a wooden spoon. Transfer to an oiled and lined 7 in (18 cm) square tin and bake at 350°F/180°C/gas mark 4 for about 30 minutes or until golden and firm to the touch.

For the topping, gently heat the honey and lemon juice. Spoon the syrup over the cake while it is still warm. Cool in the tin to allow the syrup to be absorbed.

If wished, decorate with whirls of whipped cream, quarter slices of lemon and pieces of crystallized ginger.

Makes 9 squares
***

CAROB & BANANA ROULADE

An especially light textured sponge rolled with a
creamy banana filling.

Free-range eggs 4
Unrefined brown sugar 1 oz (25 g)
Vanilla essence ½ tsp (2.5 ml)
Wholemeal flour ½ oz (15 g)
Carob powder, sieved ½ oz (15 g)
Ground almonds 2 tbsp (30 ml)

FILLING
Bananas 2
Lemon, juice of ½
Ground almonds 2 oz (50 g)
Whipping or double cream 5 tbsp (75 ml)

Whisk the eggs and sugar over a saucepan of
simmering water until very pale, thick and creamy.
Remove from the heat. Whisk in the vanilla essence,
then fold in the flour and carob powder. Transfer to a
7½×12 in (19×30 cm) Swiss roll tin lined with non-
stick paper. Bake at 350°F/180°C/gas mark 4 for 15–
20 minutes. The sponge should spring back when
lightly touched.

Sprinkle a piece of non-stick paper with the ground
almonds and carefully turn out the sponge. Remove
the lining paper and then, using a knife, make an
indentation ½ in (1.5 cm) from one short edge. Roll
up from that end, leaving the paper in between. Cool
completely.

For the filling, mash the bananas with the lemon
juice. Stir in the ground almonds. Whisk the cream
until stiff, then fold into the banana mixture. Unroll
the cooled sponge and spread with the filling. Reroll
and trim the ends.

APPLE & SPICE SQUARES

Very moist and more like a pudding than a cake, these
tasty squares are popular with children. Sultanas or
chopped dried fruits may be substituted for the
walnuts.

Butter 4 oz (100 g)
Unrefined brown sugar 6 oz (175 g)
Self-raising wholemeal flour 4 oz (100 g)
Free-range egg, beaten 1
Cooking apples, cored and sliced 8 oz (225 g)
Walnuts, chopped 2 oz (50 g)
Ground cinnamon ½ tsp (2.5 ml)
Ground cloves ½ tsp (2.5 ml)

Melt the butter and add 4 oz (100 g) of the sugar. Stir
in the flour and beaten egg. Combine all the
remaining ingredients in a mixing bowl, then gently
fold into the cake mixture. Transfer to an oiled and
lined shallow 7 in (18 cm) square cake tin.

Bake at 350°F/180°C/gas mark 4 for about 40
minutes until golden brown and firm to the touch.
Cool in the tin before cutting into squares.

Makes 9 squares
***

CAROB MADEIRA CAKE

A very popular cake, made regularly in Cranks'
Bakery. As an alternative, slice and fill the centre with
sugar-free apricot jam.

Butter 6 oz (175 g)
Unrefined brown sugar 6 oz (175 g)
Free-range eggs, beaten 3
Wholemeal flour 8 oz (225 g)
Baking powder 1½ tsp (7.5 ml)
Carob powder 2 tbsp (30 ml)
Boiling water 3 tbsp (45 ml)
Milk 2 tbsp (30 ml)

Topping: *Whipping cream 4 tbsp (60 ml)*
Carob bar, broken 4 oz (100 g)
Flaked almonds, toasted, to decorate

Oil and line a 7 in (18 cm) round cake tin. Cream the
butter and sugar until very pale, light and fluffy. Beat
in the eggs a little at a time, adding 1 tbsp (15 ml) of
the measured flour if the mixture starts to curdle.

Dissolve the carob powder in the boiling water. Mix
the flour and the baking powder together and fold
into the creamed mixture with the carob liquid. Stir in
the milk to give a soft dropping consistency.

Transfer to the prepared tin, level the surface and
bake at 325°F/160°C/gas mark 3 for 1–1¼ hours. The
cake should be well risen, firm to the touch, and when
tested with a skewer it should come out clean. Cool
on a wire tray.

For the topping, heat the cream gently in a small
saucepan. Add the broken carob bar and stir until
melted and smooth. Pour over the cake, allowing it to
trickle down the sides. Sprinkle with flaked almonds.

*** without icing

STRAWBERRY LEMON COUSCOUS CAKE

This rather unusual dessert cake should be made and eaten on the same day.

BASE
Flaked almonds, toasted 2 oz (50 g)
Rolled oats, toasted 2 oz (50 g)
Butter 2 oz (50 g)
Malt extract 2 oz (50 g)

FILLING
Apple concentrate 4 fl oz (100 ml)
Water 18 fl oz (500 ml)
Couscous 8 oz (225 g)
Lemon, finely grated rind and juice of 1
Tahini 3 tbsp (45 ml)
Vanilla essence 1 tsp (5 ml)
Malt extract 2 tbsp (30 ml)
Sugar-free strawberry jam 4 oz (100 g)

TOPPING AND DECORATION
Water ½ pt (300 ml)
Apple concentrate 2 tbsp (30 ml)
Agar flakes 1 tbsp (15 ml)
Lemon, finely grated rind of 1
Fresh strawberries, sliced 8 oz (225 g)

Line an 8 in (20 cm) spring release tin with non-stick paper. For the base, combine the almonds and oats. Heat the butter and malt extract together until just bubbling. Add the oat mixture, stir well and press on to the base of the prepared tin. Chill.

Place the apple concentrate and water in a saucepan, add the couscous. Heat gently, cover and simmer for 3–5 minutes until the liquid is absorbed, stirring occasionally to prevent sticking.

Remove from the heat and stir in the lemon rind and juice, tahini, vanilla essence and malt extract. Allow to stand for 20 minutes. Spread the jam over the base and spoon the couscous mixture on top. Level the surface and chill.

For the topping, place the water, apple concentrate and agar flakes in a small saucepan. Bring to the boil, then simmer for about 5 minutes. Stir in the lemon rind and chill until beginning to set. Meanwhile, decorate the top of the cake with the sliced strawberries. Spoon the lemon glaze carefully over the strawberries and chill until set.

OLD FASHIONED SEED CAKE

Butter 6 oz (175 g)
Unrefined brown sugar 6 oz (175 g)
Free-range eggs, beaten 3
Wholemeal flour 8 oz (225 g)
Baking powder 1 tsp (5 ml)
Caraway seeds 2 tsp (10 ml)
Ground cinnamon ½ tsp (2.5 ml)
Ground cloves ½ tsp (2.5 ml)
Milk 2–3 tbsp (30–45 ml)

Cream the butter and sugar until pale and fluffy. Gradually beat in the eggs. Mix the flour, baking powder, caraway seeds and spices thoroughly, then fold into the mixture with sufficient milk to give a soft dropping consistency. Transfer to a buttered and lined 7 in (18 cm) round cake tin, level the surface and bake at 350°F/180°C/gas mark 4 for 1–1¼ hours or until golden and springy to the touch. Cool on a wire tray.

***

STICKY DATE GINGERBREAD

Butter 4 oz (100 g)
Unrefined brown sugar 4 oz (100 g)
Malt extract 4 oz (100 g)
Molasses 4 oz (100 g)
Milk ¼ pt (150 ml)
Dried dates, stoned and chopped 3 oz (75 g)
Wholemeal flour 8 oz (225 g)
Bicarbonate of soda ½ tsp (2.5 ml)
Baking powder 1 tsp (5 ml)
Ground ginger 2 tsp (10 ml)
Ground cinnamon 1 tsp (5 ml)
Free-range egg, beaten 1

Melt the butter, sugar, malt extract, molasses and milk together over a gentle heat. Add the chopped dates. Allow to cool slightly then mix in the flour, bicarbonate of soda, baking powder, ginger, cinnamon and egg and beat well. Transfer the mixture to an oiled and lined 11×7 in (28×18 cm) shallow cake tin and bake at 325°F/160°C/gas mark 3 for about 30 minutes, until just firm to the touch. Allow to cool in the tin before cutting into squares.

Makes 15 squares
***

CHECKERBOARD CAKE

This is a Cranks variation of the traditional
Battenburg Cake.

Butter 6 oz (175 g)
Unrefined brown sugar 6oz (175 g)
Free-range eggs, beaten 3
Almond essence, a few drops
Self-raising wholemeal flour 5½ oz (165 g)
Carob powder, sieved ½ oz (15 g)
Apricot jam 6 tbsp (90 ml)
Almond paste, 1 quantity (see p. 88)

Oil and line a 7 in (18 cm) square cake tin. Divide in
half with a piece of thin card covered with foil. Cream
the butter and sugar until light and fluffy. Gradually
beat in the eggs, then divide the mixture in half. Add
the almond essence and 3 oz (75 g) flour to one half.
Fold the remaining flour and the carob powder into
the other half. Transfer one mixture to each side of the
prepared tin and level the surface. Bake at 350°F/
180°C/gas mark 4 for about 40–45 minutes until well
risen and springy to the touch. Cool on a wire tray.

Cut each cake in half lengthways and trim the sides.
Sandwich the strips together with apricot jam,
alternating the colours.

Roll out the almond paste so that the width is as
long as the cake and the length will wrap round to
enclose the cake completely. Spread a little jam over
the almond paste and wrap around the assembled
Checkerboard Cake, sealing the join well. To give a
decorative finish, mark a lattice pattern on the top
with a knife and crimp the edges.

WALNUT, CINNAMON & HONEY CAKE

Best eaten on the day of making.

Butter 4 oz (100 g)
Unrefined brown sugar 2 oz (50 g)
Honey 2 oz (50 g)
Free-range eggs, beaten 2
Self-raising wholemeal flour 4 oz (100 g)
Ground cinnamon 1 tsp (5 ml)
Walnuts, chopped 3 oz (75 g)
Honey to glaze

SAUCE (optional)
Thick Greek yoghourt ⅓ pt (200 ml)
Soured cream 4 fl oz (100 ml)
Ground cinnamon 1½ tsp (7.5 ml)

Cream the butter, sugar and honey until light and fluffy. Beat in the eggs gradually, then fold in the flour, cinnamon and 2 oz (50 g) of the chopped walnuts. Transfer to an oiled and base-lined shallow 7½ in (19 cm) square cake tin. Level the surface and bake at 375°F/190°C/gas mark 5 for 20–25 minutes until golden and springy to the touch. Cool on a wire tray. Brush with honey to glaze and sprinkle with the remaining walnuts. Cut into squares.

For the sauce, stir the yoghourt, soured cream and cinnamon together and serve separately.

Makes 9 squares
***

MINCEMEAT TURNABOUT TRIANGLES

TOPPING
Butter 1 oz (25 g)
Cranks fruit mincemeat (see p. 85) 6 tbsp (90 ml)

CAKE
Butter 3 oz (75 g)
Self-raising wholemeal flour 8 oz (225 g)
Salt, a pinch
Unrefined brown sugar 3 oz (75 g)
Lemon, finely grated rind and juice of ½
Milk, just under ¼ pt (150 ml)
Free-range egg, beaten 1

Butter and base-line a shallow 7½ in (19 cm) square cake tin. Beat the butter and mincemeat together and spread over the base of the tin.

For the cake, rub the butter into the flour and salt, then stir in the sugar and lemon rind. Make the lemon juice up to ¼ pt (150 ml) with milk, then stir into the mixture with the beaten egg to make a soft dropping consistency. Spread evenly over the mincemeat. Bake at 350°F/180°C/gas mark 4 for about 30 minutes until golden and well risen. Cool slightly in the tin before turning out on to a plate. Cool and serve cut into triangles.

Makes 8 triangles
***

CHRISTMAS CAKE

Cranks' favourite recipe which is used every year and can be made months in advance. Try it covered with apricot marzipan (see p. 88).

Sultanas 8 oz (225 g)
Raisins 8 oz (225 g)
Currants 2½ oz (65 g)
Dried apricots, chopped 2½ oz (65 g)
Sherry or brandy 4 tbsp (60 ml)
Orange, finely grated rind and juice of 1
Lemon, finely grated rind and juice of 1
Butter 6 oz (175 g)
Unrefined brown sugar 8 oz (225 g)
Free-range eggs, beaten 3
Vanilla essence 1 tsp (5 ml)
Walnuts, chopped 1½ oz (40 g)
Almonds, chopped 1½ oz (40 g)
Wholemeal flour 8 oz (225 g)
Ground mixed spice 1 tsp (5 ml)
Ground nutmeg ½ tsp (2.5 ml)
Ground ginger ½ tsp (2.5 ml)
Sherry or brandy – for maturing

Soak the sultanas, raisins, currants and apricots in the sherry, with the orange and lemon rind and juice overnight.

Butter and line an 8½ in (21.5 cm) cake tin with a double layer of greaseproof paper. Tie a double thickness of brown paper round the tin.

Cream the butter and sugar until very pale and fluffy. Gradually beat in the eggs and vanilla essence. Combine all the remaining ingredients in a separate bowl, then stir into the creamed mixture alternately with the soaked fruit. Transfer to the prepared tin and make a slight hollow in the centre.

Bake at 325°F/160°C/gas mark 3 for 1 hour then reduce to 275°F/140°C/gas mark 1 for a further 1½ hours or until a skewer inserted comes out clean. Cover the top of the cake with a circle of greaseproof paper if necessary for the last ¾ hour. Allow to cool slightly in the tin before transferring to a wire tray.

Sprinkle liberally with sherry or brandy. Wrap in fresh greaseproof paper and store in an airtight tin or foil to mature. To ensure a moist cake, sprinkle with more sherry or brandy from time to time.

***

STICKY MALTED PRUNE & SPICE CAKE

Prunes 4 oz (100 g)
Malt extract 4 oz (100 g)
Vegetable oil 4 fl oz (100 ml)
Free-range eggs 2
Wholemeal flour 5 oz (150 g)
Bicarbonate of soda ½ tsp (2.5 ml)
Ground cinnamon 1 tsp (5 ml)
Ground mixed spice ½ tsp (2.5 ml)
Ground nutmeg ½ tsp (2.5 ml)
Ground cloves, a pinch
Natural yoghourt or buttermilk 4 fl oz (100 ml)

TOPPING
Natural yoghourt or buttermilk 3 tbsp (45 ml)
Milk 1 tbsp (15 ml)
Molasses 1 tbsp (15 ml)
Vanilla essence ½ tsp (2.5 ml)

Just cover the prunes with water in a small saucepan. Bring to the boil and simmer for 10–15 minutes until tender. Drain, remove the stones and chop.

Whisk the malt extract, oil and eggs until thick and smooth, then stir in the chopped prunes and remaining ingredients. Pour into a buttered and lined shallow 8 in (20 cm) square cake tin and bake at 350°F/180°C/gas mark 4 for about 30 minutes, until risen and firm to the touch.

For the topping, heat all the ingredients gently in a small pan. Prick the top of the cake with a skewer and spoon over the sauce, allowing it to soak into the cake. Cool in the tin.

Serve cut into squares.

Makes 9 squares
***

STICKY FIG
& ALMOND CAKE

This gooey cake is absolutely delicious. Serve it cut
into squares.

Dried figs, chopped 4 oz (100 g)
Unrefined brown sugar 4 oz (100 g)
Vegetable oil 4 fl oz (100 ml)
Free-range eggs 2
Almond essence 3–4 drops
Wholemeal flour 3 oz (75 g)
Ground almonds 2 oz (50 g)
Bicarbonate of soda ½ tsp (2.5 ml)
Natural yoghourt or buttermilk 4 fl oz (100 ml)

TOPPING
Maple syrup 3 tbsp (45 ml)
Natural yoghourt or buttermilk 3 tbsp (45 ml)
Flaked almonds, toasted ½ oz (15 g)

Just cover the figs with water and simmer for about 5
minutes until soft. Drain. Whisk the sugar, oil and
eggs until pale, thick and creamy, then whisk in the
almond essence. Mix in the flour, ground almonds
and bicarbonate of soda. Beat well, then fold in the
figs and the yoghourt or buttermilk. Turn into a
buttered and lined 7 in (18 cm) square shallow tin and
bake at 350°F/180°C/gas mark 4 for about 45 minutes
until well risen, golden and springy to the touch.

For the topping, gently heat the maple syrup and
yoghourt in a small saucepan. Spoon over the warm
cake and allow to soak in. Cool in the tin. Sprinkle
with the toasted flaked almonds.

Makes 9 squares
***

TRADITIONAL DUNDEE CAKE

Whole almonds, blanched 4 oz (100 g)
Butter 8 oz (225 g)
Unrefined brown sugar 8 oz (225 g)
Orange, finely grated rind of 1
Lemon, finely grated rind of 1
Free-range eggs, beaten 4
Wholemeal flour 8 oz (225 g)
Baking powder 1 tsp (5 ml)
Salt, a pinch
Ground mixed spice ½ tsp (2.5 ml)
Sultanas 6 oz (175 g)
Currants 6 oz (175 g)
Raisins 6 oz (175 g)

Butter and line a 7 in (18 cm) round cake tin. Chop 1 oz (25 g) of the almonds, reserving the remainder for the top of the cake. Cream the butter and sugar until pale and fluffy. Beat in the orange and lemon rinds, then gradually beat in the eggs. Combine the flour, baking powder, salt and mixed spice and alternately fold into the mixture with the dried fruits and chopped nuts.

Transfer to the prepared tin, level the surface and decorate with the whole almonds. Bake at 325°F/160°C/gas mark 3 for 1 hour. Reduce the temperature to 300°F/150°C/gas mark 2 for a further 1–1½ hours or until an inserted skewer comes out clean. Leave in the tin for 15 minutes before transferring on to a wire tray.

***

BOIL AND BAKE
FRUIT & NUT CAKE

This moist and fruity cake is very easy to make
and keeps well.

Currants 4 oz (100 g)
Raisins 4 oz (100 g)
Sultanas 4 oz (100 g)
Dried dates, stoned and chopped 3 oz (75 g)
Dried apricots, chopped 3 oz (75 g)
Prunes, pitted 2 oz (50 g)
Unrefined brown sugar 4 oz (100 g)
Orange, finely grated rind of 1
Orange juice 1/4 pt (150 ml)
Apricot jam 4 oz (100 g)
Butter 8 oz (225 g)
Free-range eggs, beaten 3
Sherry or brandy 2 tbsp (30 ml)
Self-raising wholemeal flour 8 oz (225 g)
Ground mixed spice 1 tsp (5 ml)
Ground cinnamon 1 tsp (5 ml)
Ground ginger 1 tsp (5 ml)
Almonds, blanched or walnuts, chopped 2 oz (50 g)
Sunflower seeds 2 oz (50 g)
Apricot jam to glaze

Place the dried fruits, sugar, orange rind and juice,
jam and butter in a saucepan. Heat, stirring to melt the
butter, then simmer for 1 minute. Allow to cool, then
beat in the eggs, sherry and dry ingredients. Transfer
to an oiled and double lined 8 in (20 cm) round cake
tin. Bake at 325°F/160°C/gas mark 3 for 45 minutes,
then reduce the temperature to 300°F/150°C/gas
mark 2 for a further 1 hour or until a skewer inserted
comes out clean. While still hot, brush the surface
with a little warmed and sieved apricot jam, then cool
in the tin.

***

TIPSY ORANGE CIDER LOAF

Delicious on its own but even better sliced and served
with butter!

Self-raising wholemeal flour 12 oz (350 g)
Sultanas 4 oz (100 g)
Raisins 4 oz (100 g)
Ground mixed spice 1 tsp (5 ml)
Butter 4 oz (100 g)
Unrefined brown sugar 4 oz (100 g)
Milk ¼ pt (150 ml)
Cider ¼ pt (150 ml)
Free-range egg, beaten 1
Orange, finely grated rind of 1

TOPPING
Unrefined brown sugar 2 oz (50 g)
Cider 2 tbsp (30 ml)
Orange juice 2 tbsp (30 ml)

Mix together the flour, sultanas, raisins and mixed
spice. Melt the butter and add the sugar. Combine the
milk and cider; the liquid will curdle. Pour this into
the dry ingredients with the beaten egg and grated
orange rind. Finally, add the melted butter and sugar
and mix well.

Transfer to an oiled and base-lined 2 lb (900 g) loaf
tin. Bake at 350°F/180°C/gas mark 4 for 30 minutes,
then reduce the temperature to 325°F/160°C/gas
mark 3 for a further 40 minutes.

For the topping, warm the sugar, cider and orange
juice. Prick the surface of the cake with a fine skewer
and spoon the syrup over, allowing it to soak in. Cool
in the tin.

***

LEMON RICE CAKE

A light and crumbly short textured cake.

Butter 8 oz (225 g)
Unrefined brown sugar 6 oz (175 g)
Lemon, finely grated rind and juice of 1
Free-range eggs, beaten 4
Self-raising wholemeal flour 8 oz (225 g)
Brown rice flour 8 oz (225 g)

Cream the butter and sugar until very light and fluffy.
Add the grated lemon rind, then gradually beat in the
eggs. Mix in the flour and rice flour and add the
lemon juice to give a soft dropping consistency.

Transfer to a buttered and lined 8 in (20 cm) round
cake tin, level the surface and bake at 325°F/160°C/
gas mark 3 until golden, well risen and springy to the
touch. Cool on a wire tray.   1 hour 25 minutes

***

31

MALT & APPLE LOAF

This moist fruited loaf is both sugar-free and suitable for those on a vegan diet.

Sultanas 3 oz (75 g)
Raisins 3 oz (75 g)
Water ½ pt (300 ml)
Lemon juice 1 tbsp (15 ml)
Apple concentrate 2 tbsp (30 ml)
Margarine 2 oz (50 g)
Malt extract 2 oz (50 g)
Wholemeal flour 10 oz (300 g)
Bicarbonate of soda ½ tsp (2.5 ml)
Ground mixed spice 1 tsp (5 ml)
Ground cloves ½ tsp (2.5 ml)

Soak the sultanas and raisins in the water, lemon juice and apple concentrate overnight.

Transfer the soaked fruit and liquid to a saucepan. Add the margarine and malt extract and heat gently to melting point. Combine the dry ingredients, then stir into the warmed mixture until thoroughly incorporated. Transfer to an oiled and base-lined 1 lb (450 g) loaf tin and bake at 325°F/160°C/gas mark 3 for 1–1¼ hours or until a skewer inserted comes out clean.

Cool on a wire tray.

***

CRANKS CARROT LOAF CAKE

Free-range eggs 2
Unrefined brown sugar 8 oz (225 g)
Vegetable oil ¼ pt (150 ml)
Milk 4 tbsp (60 ml)
Self-raising wholemeal flour 8 oz (225 g)
Ground cinnamon 1 tsp (5 ml)
Ground nutmeg 1 tsp (5 ml)
Desiccated coconut 2 oz (50 g)
Raisins 5 oz (150 g)
Carrots, finely grated 10 oz (300 g)

Whisk the eggs and sugar until very thick and creamy.
Whisk in the oil and then the milk. Mix in the
remaining ingredients and transfer to a buttered and
base-lined 2 lb (900 g) loaf tin. Bake at 350°F/180°C/
gas mark 4 for about 1¼–1½ hours until risen and
firm to the touch.

Cool on a wire tray.

***

BANANA LOAF CAKE

Butter 5 oz (150 g)
Self-raising wholemeal flour 10 oz (300 g)
Unrefined brown sugar 5 oz (150 g)
Sultanas 2 oz (50 g)
Walnuts, chopped 1 oz (25 g)
Bananas (peeled weight), mashed 1 lb (450 g)
Free-range eggs 2

Rub the butter into the flour until the mixture
resembles fine crumbs. Add the sugar, sultanas and
chopped walnuts. Whisk the bananas and eggs
together until very thick and creamy, then fold in the
dry ingredients. Transfer to an oiled and base-lined
2 lb (900 g) loaf tin and bake at 350°F/180°C/gas
mark 4 for about 1¼–1½ hours, until risen and firm to
the touch.

Cool on a wire tray.

PARKIN

Butter 2 oz (50 g)
Nutter 2 oz (50 g)
Unrefined brown sugar 4 oz (100 g)
Molasses 6 oz (175 g)
Honey 6 oz (175 g)
Wholemeal flour 8 oz (225 g)
Coarse oatmeal 8 oz (225 g)
Baking powder 2 tsp (10 ml)
Ground ginger 1 tsp (5 ml)
Ground mixed spice 1 tsp (5 ml)
Salt, a pinch
Milk or soya milk 4 tbsp (60 ml)

Melt the butter, nutter, sugar, molasses and honey
together in a pan over a gentle heat. Remove from the
heat, add the remaining ingredients and beat lightly
with a wooden spoon until thoroughly mixed.
Transfer to an oiled and lined 11×7 in (28×18 cm)
cake tin and bake at 350°F/180°C/gas mark 4 for
about 45 minutes until just firm to the touch. Cool on
a wire tray.

Do not remove the paper, but wrap in foil and store
in an airtight container for several days. Cut into bars
to serve.

Makes 12 bars
***

BAKEWELL SLICES

This is based on the traditional Bakewell recipe. It is thought to have originated when a Bakewell cook made a mistake and put ground almonds in her sponge mixture instead of flour!

*Wholemeal pastry made using wholemeal flour 7 oz (200 g)
(see chart, p. 92)
Strawberry or raspberry jam 6 tbsp (90 ml)
Free-range eggs 4
Unrefined brown sugar 4 oz (100 g)
Ground almonds 4 oz (100 g)
Butter, melted 4 oz (100 g)
Flaked almonds 1 oz (25 g)*

Line an 11×7 in (28×18 cm) cake tin with the pastry. Spread the base with jam. Whisk the eggs and sugar over a saucepan of simmering water until pale and thick and the whisk leaves a trail in the mixture. Fold the ground almonds into the whisked mixture and finally fold in the melted butter. Pour into the pastry case and sprinkle with the flaked almonds. Bake at 400°F/200°C/gas mark 6 for 25–30 minutes, or until risen, golden and set. Cool in the tin before cutting into slices.

Makes 12 slices
***

FRUITY NUT BARS

An ideal and tasty bar for children – it is also sugar-free and suitable for vegans.

Sultanas 2 oz (50 g)
Raisins 2 oz (50 g)
Currants 2 oz (50 g)
Water ¾ pt (450 ml)
Apple concentrate 5 tbsp (75 ml)
Wholemeal flour 2½ oz (65 g)
Rolled oats 8 oz (225 g)
Broken cashew nuts 4 oz (100 g)
Walnuts, chopped 4 oz (100 g)
Cooking apple, cored and diced 1 large

TOPPING
Apple and pear spread 4 tbsp (60 ml)
Apple concentrate 2 tbsp (30 ml)

Soak the sultanas, raisins and currants in the water and apple concentrate overnight.

Stir in the remaining ingredients and transfer to an oiled 11×7 in (28×18 cm) cake tin. Level the surface and bake at 325°F/160°C/gas mark 3 for 50–60 minutes. Cool in the tin.

Combine the apple and pear spread with the apple concentrate. Brush over the cooled surface before cutting into bars.

Makes 12 bars

ORANGE GINGER ROCK CAKES

Sugarless and vegan, this recipe is a variation of the traditional rock cakes. Best eaten fresh. Sugar (2–3 oz/50–75 g) may be added to give a sweeter, crisper result.

Large orange, finely grated rind and juice of 1
Dried dates, stoned 8 oz (225 g)
Margarine 8 oz (225 g)
Soya milk 4 fl oz (100 ml)
Self-raising wholemeal flour 1 lb (450 g)
Sultanas 4 oz (100 g)
Raisins 4 oz (100 g)
Flaked almonds 4 oz (100 g)
Ground ginger ½ tsp (2.5 ml)
Ground mixed spice ½ tsp (2.5 ml)

Make the orange juice up to 4 fl oz (100 ml) with water if necessary and pour into a small saucepan. Add the dates and simmer until soft and pulpy. Cool.

Beat the margarine and cooled dates until very light and fluffy. Add the grated orange rind and gradually mix in the soya milk.

In a mixing bowl, combine the remaining ingredients, then gently fold into the creamed mixture. Place large "rocky" heaps on to a buttered baking tray. Bake at 350°F/180°C/gas mark 4 for about 20 minutes until just golden. Cool on a wire tray.

Makes 15
***

MAIDS OF HONOUR

These famous little cakes date back to the 16th century. Their name is said to be derived from the maids of honour attending Queen Elizabeth I and those of Henry VIII. There are many versions, this one uses Lebnie instead of the traditional curds made with rennet.

Cranks puff pastry ¼ quantity (see p. 90)
Lebnie 4 oz (100 g) (see p. 9)
Butter 2 oz (50 g)
Egg yolks 2
Brandy 1 tbsp (15 ml)
Unrefined brown sugar 2 oz (50 g)
Lemon 1
Ground cinnamon, a pinch
Ground nutmeg, a pinch
Ground almonds 1 oz (25 g)
Currants 1 oz (25 g)

Roll out the pastry thinly and, using a 3 in (7.5 cm) fluted cutter, stamp out 12 rounds. Use to line patty tins.

Blend the Lebnie and butter together in a liquidizer or food processor. Add the egg yolks, brandy, sugar, finely grated rind from the lemon and ½ the juice, spices and ground almonds. Blend well, then stir in the currants.

Spoon the filling into the pastry cases and bake at 400°F/200°C/gas mark 6 for about 15 minutes until the pastry is well risen and the filling set and golden.

Best served warm.

If Lebnie is difficult to obtain, in this recipe curd cheese may be substituted.

Makes 12

ECCLES CAKES

The addition of lemon juice to this filling helps to balance the richness of the dried fruit.

Cranks puff pastry ½ quantity (see p. 90)
Butter 2 oz (50 g)
Unrefined brown sugar 2 oz (50 g)
Currants 4 oz (100 g)
Sultanas 4 oz (100 g)
Lemon, juice of 1
Egg white, beaten, to glaze
Unrefined Demerara sugar, to glaze

Roll out the pastry ¼ in (6 mm) thick and stamp out 4 in (10 cm) rounds. Beat the butter and sugar until pale and fluffy, mix in the currants, sultanas and lemon juice.

Place heaped teaspoons of the mixture in the centre of each pastry round, dampen the edges, then draw up and pinch together to encase the filling. Turn the cakes over and flatten each to about 2½ in (6.5 cm); the fruit should just show through the pastry. Score the tops with a diamond pattern and place on baking trays, sprinkled with water.

To glaze, brush each one with lightly-beaten egg white and sprinkle with sugar. Bake at 425°F/220°C/ gas mark 7 for about 15–20 minutes until puffed up and golden.

Best served warm.

Makes 16–20
***

LUSCIOUS LEMON TARTLETS
WITH ALMOND MERINGUE

These tartlets are absolutely irresistible!

Wholemeal pastry made with wholemeal flour
6 oz (175 g) (see chart, p. 92) or Rich wholemeal shortcrust
pastry 1 quantity (see p. 89)
Cranks raw sugar lemon curd 12 tsp (60 ml) (see p. 86)
Egg whites 2
Unrefined brown sugar 4 oz (100 g)
Almond essence ½ tsp (2.5 ml)
Toasted flaked almonds 1½ oz (40 g)

Roll out the pastry and, using a 3 in (7.5 cm) fluted
cutter, stamp out 12 rounds, use to line patty tins.
Spoon 1 tsp (5 ml) lemon curd into each pastry case.

Whisk the egg whites until stiff, whisk in the sugar a
little at a time and then the almond essence. Continue
whisking for about 30 seconds until thick and glossy.

Top each lemon tartlet with meringue and sprinkle
with flaked almonds. Bake at 350°F/180°C/gas mark 4
for about 20 minutes.

Makes 12

MARMALADE CUP CAKES

A variety of interesting little cakes can be made from
a basic sponge mixture. Bake them in patty tins or
individual paper cases.

Butter 4 oz (100 g)
Unrefined brown sugar 4 oz (100 g)
Free-range eggs, beaten 2
Self-raising wholemeal flour 4 oz (100 g)
Marmalade 1 tbsp (15 ml)
Shreds of orange peel to decorate
Marmalade to glaze

Cream the butter and sugar until pale and fluffy. Beat
in the eggs a little at a time. Fold in the flour and the
marmalade. Spoon the mixture into buttered or paper
case lined patty tins. Set two small strips of orange
peel into the top of each bun. Bake at 375°F/190°C/
gas mark 5 for about 15 minutes until well risen,
golden and springy to the touch. Cool on a wire tray,
then brush with warmed marmalade to glaze.

Variations
Lemon & Caraway Cup Cakes
Substitute the grated rind of 1 lemon and 1 tsp (5 ml)
caraway seeds for the marmalade. If wished, glaze by
brushing with 1 tbsp (15 ml) lemon curd, warmed
together with 1 tbsp (15 ml) water.

Carob Cup Cakes with Carob Icing
Substitute ½ oz (15 g) sieved carob powder for ½ oz
(15 g) of the flour. Use ginger or lime marmalade to
glaze. For the icing melt 2 oz (50 g) carob chip or
broken carob bar with 2 tbsp (30 ml) whipping cream
and use to decorate the cup cakes.

Makes 12–15
***

ORANGE & SUNFLOWER SLICES WITH DATES

The natural sweetness of dates and orange juice are used to sweeten these unusual slices.

Dried dates, stoned 6 oz (175 g)
Water ¼ pt (150 ml)
Butter 3 oz (75 g)
Vegetable oil 4 tbsp (60 ml)
Free-range eggs, beaten 2
Orange, finely grated rind of 1
Orange juice 4 tbsp (60 ml)
Wholemeal flour 8 oz (225 g)
Desiccated coconut 4 oz (100 g)
Millet flakes 2 oz (50 g)
Sultanas 2 oz (50 g)
Sunflower seeds 2 oz (50 g)

Simmer the dates in the water to a soft purée. Cool. Cream the dates and the butter until light and fluffy, then beat in the oil a little at a time. Gradually beat in the eggs, then the orange rind and juice. Add the remaining ingredients and stir until evenly mixed. Transfer to an oiled 11×7 in (28×18 cm) shallow cake tin and bake at 350°F/180°C/gas mark 4 for 20–25 minutes. Cool in the tin then cut into slices.

Makes 12 slices
***

APRICOT & CASHEW NUT BARS

These rather unusual sugar-free squares have a chewy, moist texture and are suitable for vegans.

Dried apricots, soaked overnight 8 oz (225 g)
Vegetable oil 4 fl oz (100 ml)
Vanilla essence 1 tsp (5 ml)
Cashew nut pieces 3 oz (75 g)
Desiccated coconut 3 oz (75 g)
Rolled oats 3 oz (75 g)
Raisins 3 oz (75 g)
Lemon, finely grated rind of 1
Ground cinnamon ½ tsp (2.5 ml)
Ground nutmeg, a pinch

Simmer the apricots in their soaking water for five minutes. Drain and cool. Whisk the cooked apricots with the oil until very smooth. Mix in all the remaining ingredients. Transfer to an oiled and base-lined 11×7 in (28×18 cm) cake tin and bake at 400°F/200°C/gas mark 6 for about 20–25 minutes until firm to the touch. Cool in the tin, then cut into bars.

Makes 12 bars
***

YORKSHIRE MAPLE SYRUP TARTLETS

Wholemeal pastry made with wholemeal flour
6 oz (175 g) (see chart, p. 92)
Dessert apple, cored and grated 1
Lemon, finely grated rind and juice of ½
Wholemeal breadcrumbs 2 oz (50 g)
Ground cinnamon, a pinch
Sultanas 1 oz (25 g)
Maple syrup 4 fl oz (100 ml)

Roll out the pastry thinly and, using a 3 in (7.5 cm) fluted cutter, stamp out 12 rounds and use to line patty tins. Mix the remaining ingredients together and spoon into the pastry cases. Bake at 375°F/190°C/gas mark 5 for about 25 minutes or until just set.

Variation
Banana Maple Syrup Tartlets
Substitute one large or two small mashed bananas for the apple, and ground ginger for the cinnamon. Add 1 tbsp (15 ml) rum.

Makes 12
***

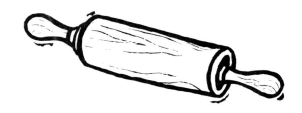

STRAWBERRY PALMIERS

Cranks puff pastry ¼ quantity (see p. 90)
Unrefined Demerara sugar 3 oz (75 g)
Whipping cream 4 fl oz (100 ml)
Strawberries, quartered or halved to decorate

Sprinkle the work surface with some of the sugar.
Roll out the pastry to a rectangle about 12×8 in
(30×20 cm) then sprinkle generously with sugar. Fold
the long sides to the centre, sprinkle with sugar, then
fold long sides together to form a long strip. Roll out
again to the original size and sprinkle with the
remaining sugar. Roll in each short side to the centre
to form a double scroll. Press well together. Trim the
ends, then cut across into ½ in (1.5 cm) slices. Place
cut side down, slightly flattened and well apart on a
baking tray sprinkled with water.

Bake at 425°F/220°C/gas mark 7 for about 5–7
minutes, then carefully turn over and cook the other
side for a further 5–7 minutes. Cool on a wire tray.

Whisk the cream and pipe on to half the biscuits.
Decorate with the strawberries, then top with the
remaining palmiers.

Variation
Lemon Cinnamon Palmiers
Mix 1 tsp (5 ml) ground cinnamon with the sugar
before rolling in. Sandwich the palmiers together with
lemon curd folded into whipped cream.

Makes 8
*** without filling

COCONUT BUNS

These buns can be left plain or decorated with raw sugar icing (see p. 36) and sprinkled with toasted coconut.

Desiccated coconut 2 oz (50 g)
Boiling water 4 fl oz (100 ml)
Vanilla essence ½ tsp (2.5 ml)
Self-raising wholemeal flour 8 oz (225 g)
Salt, a pinch
Butter 3 oz (75 g)
Unrefined brown sugar 3 oz (75 g)
Free-range egg, beaten 1
Egg white or milk to glaze
Desiccated coconut to decorate

Soak the coconut in the boiling water with the vanilla essence for about 15 minutes. Place the flour and salt in a bowl. Rub in the butter until the mixture resembles fine crumbs, then stir in the sugar. Add the egg and the coconut mixture and mix to give a fairly stiff consistency.

Divide the mixture between 12 paper cases set in patty tins. Brush with egg white or milk and sprinkle with extra coconut. Bake at 400°F/200°C/gas mark 6 for about 20 minutes until golden. Cool on a wire tray.

Makes 12
***

APPLE STRUDEL

Based on the Austrian recipe, Cranks uses puff pastry instread of strudel leaves. Serve this delicious tea time treat either warm or cold with clotted cream!

Cranks puff pastry ¼ quantity (see p. 90)
Unrefined brown sugar 1½ oz (40 g)
Ground almonds 1 oz (25 g)
Almonds, chopped 2 oz (50 g)
Sultanas 2 oz (50 g)
Ground cinnamon 1 tsp (5 ml)
Lemon, finely grated rind of 1
Cooking apples, cored and grated 2
Egg white, beaten, to glaze
Unrefined brown sugar, to sprinkle

Roll out the pastry thinly to a rectangle 16×14 in (40×35 cm). For the filling, mix all the remaining ingredients and spread over the pastry, leaving a 1 in (2.5 cm) border. Fold in the border, then roll up from a short side. Place on an oiled baking tray. Brush with lightly beaten egg white and sprinkle with sugar. Bake at 425°F/220°C/gas mark 7 for about 20–25 minutes or until golden brown and crispy.

***

Mincemeat Turnabout Triangles, page 23
Carob & Banana Roulade, page 15
Marmalade Cup Cakes, page 42
Coffee & Walnut Fingers, page 55
Celery Cheese Sables, page 63
Strawberry Palmiers, page 46

Coconut Raspberry Macaroons, page 49
Walnut, Cinnamon & Honey Cake, page 22
Pecan Fudge Brownies, page 50
Honey Shortbread, page 61
Triple Layer Orange Gâteau, page 83

Orange Ginger Rock Cakes, page 38
Blackcurrant Carob Choux Ring, page 76
Carob Madeira Cake, page 17
Banana & Peanut Cookies, page 72
Maple Snaps, page 59
Millet & Almond Cookies, page 73

Soft Bake Muesli Apple Cookies, page 56
Coffee & Walnut Cream Ring, page 81
Gingerbread Men, page 66
Yorkshire Maple Syrup Tartlets, page 45
Sticky Fig & Almond Cake, page 27

Checkerboard Cake, page 21
Oatmeal Biscuits, page 68
Pop Corn Chews, page 58
Maids of Honour, page 39
Rum & Raisin Tofu Cake, page 78

Orange Cream Kisses, page 65
Jammy Double Deckers, page 64
Honey, Lemon & Ginger Squares, page 14
Fruity Nut Bars, page 37
Strawberry Lemon Couscous Cake, page 18

Traditional Dundee Cake, page 28
Hazelnut, Coffee & Raspberry Gâteau, page 82
Luscious Lemon Tartlets with Almond Meringue, page 41
Valentine Biscuits, page 67
Honey Florentines, page 57

COCONUT RASPBERRY MACAROONS

Coconut pyramids with a difference!

Egg whites 2
Unrefined brown sugar 4 oz (100 g)
Sugar-free raspberry jam 2 tbsp (30 ml)
Desiccated coconut 8 oz (225 g)

Whisk the egg whites until stiff. Whisk in the sugar a little at a time. Then fold in the jam and coconut. Shape the mixture into nine pyramids well apart on a baking sheet covered with rice paper or non-stick paper. Bake at 325°F/160°C/gas mark 3 for about 45 minutes until golden. Cool on a wire tray.

Makes 9
***

PECAN FUDGE BROWNIES

Deliciously rich and spongy brownies, made extra special with pecans and carob topping.

Free-range eggs 3
Unrefined brown sugar 5 oz (150 g)
Salt 1/4 tsp (1.25 ml)
Vanilla essence 1 tsp (5 ml)
Carob chips, or bars, broken 3 oz (75 g)
Butter 4 oz (100 g)
Self-raising wholemeal flour 4 oz (100 g)
Sultanas 2 oz (50 g)
Pecans, roughly chopped 3 oz (75 g)

TOPPING
Carob chips, or bars, broken 3 oz (75 g)
Double cream 5 tbsp (75 ml)
Pecan halves 12

Whisk the eggs, sugar, salt and vanilla essence until pale, thick and creamy. Melt the carob chips and butter together in a bowl over a saucepan of simmering water. Stir into the whisked mixture, then fold in the flour, sultanas and chopped pecan nuts. Transfer to an oiled and base-lined 11×7 in (28×18 cm) shallow cake tin. Bake at 350°F/180°C/gas mark 4 for about 30 minutes until springy to the touch. Cool in the tin.

For the topping, melt the carob chips and cream together in a small saucepan. Pour over the cooled cake and spread evenly over the surface. Decorate with pecan halves. When set, cut into bars.

Makes 12 bars
*** without topping

APPLE & DATE SLICE

Cooking apples, cored and sliced 12 oz (350 g)
Dried dates, stoned and chopped 4 oz (100 g)
Water 6 tbsp (90 ml)
Lemon, finely grated rind and juice of 1
Ground cinnamon ½ tsp (2.5 ml)
Ground cloves, a generous pinch
Wholemeal flour 8 oz (225 g)
Rolled oats 4 oz (100 g)
Unrefined brown sugar 3 oz (75 g)
Butter, melted 5 oz (150 g)

Simmer the sliced apples and dates in the water with
the lemon rind and juice until soft. Add the cinnamon
and cloves. Combine the remaining ingredients and
press half of this mixture into a buttered 11×7 in
(28×18 cm) cake tin. Cover with the fruit mixture,
then sprinkle the remaining crumble on top. Press
down lightly. Bake at 400°F/200°C/gas mark 6 for 20
minutes.

Cool in the tin before cutting into slices.

Makes 12 slices
***

MINCE PIES

Wholemeal pastry made with wholemeal flour
9 oz (250 g) (see chart, p. 92)
or Cranks puff pastry ¼ quantity (see p. 90)
Cranks fruit mincemeat 8–10 oz (225–300 g) (see p. 85)
Egg white, beaten, to glaze
Unrefined Demerara sugar, to sprinkle

Roll out the pastry thinly and stamp out bases and lids
using 3 in (7.5 cm) and 2½ in (6.5 cm) fluted cutters.
Line patty tins with the pastry bases. Spoon a little
mincemeat into each case and top with the lids
brushed with water at the edges and seal well. Glaze
with beaten egg white and sprinkle with sugar. Make
a small slit in the top of each one. Bake at 400°F/
200°C/gas mark 6 for about 20 minutes. If using puff
pastry, bake at 425°F/220°C/gas mark 7 for about 15
minutes or until risen and golden.

Makes 12
***

MELTING MOMENTS

Butter 2 oz (50 g)
Nutter 2 oz (50 g)
Unrefined brown sugar 3 oz (75 g)
Vanilla essence ½ tsp (2.5 ml)
Self-raising wholemeal flour 4 oz (100 g)
Rolled oats 1 oz (25 g)

Cream the fats and sugar until light and fluffy. Beat in the vanilla essence. Add the flour and rolled oats and work to an even consistency. Roll into small balls about 1 in (2.5 cm) in diameter. Place on a buttered baking tray and flatten slightly.

Bake at 350°F/180°C/gas mark 4 for 15–20 minutes. Cool on a wire tray.

Makes about 16
***

HAZELNUT MACAROONS

Rich, delicious and irresistible!

Egg whites 2
Unrefined brown sugar 3 oz (75 g)
Vanilla essence ½ tsp (2.5 ml)
Brown rice flour 1 oz (25 g)
Ground hazelnuts 3 oz (75 g)
Whole hazelnuts 1 oz (25 g)

Whisk the egg whites until fairly stiff. Whisk in the sugar a little at a time and continue whisking until the mixture is very smooth and glossy and will stand in stiff peaks. Whisk in the vanilla essence. Lightly fold in the rice flour and all the hazelnuts.

Place tablespoonfuls of the mixture on to a baking tray covered with non-stick paper. Bake at 350°F/ 180°C/gas mark 4 for 15–20 minutes or until lightly golden. Cool on a wire tray.

Variation
Carob Hazelnut Macaroons
Substitute carob chips for the whole hazelnuts.

Makes 18–20

COFFEE & WALNUT FINGERS

A variety of piped shapes can be made with this mixture. For a treat, sandwich them together with flavoured butter cream (see p. 87).

Butter 8 oz (225 g)
Unrefined brown sugar 2 oz (50 g)
Instant coffee 1 tbsp (15 ml)
Water, boiling 1 tbsp (15 ml)
Walnuts, roasted and ground 2 oz (50 g)
Self-raising wholemeal flour 8 oz (225 g)
Salt, a pinch
Milk or soya milk 3 tbsp (45 ml)

Cream the butter and sugar until very light and fluffy. Dissolve the instant coffee in the boiling water and beat into the creamed mixture. Mix in the walnuts, flour, salt, and sufficient milk to give a soft consistency. Pipe "fingers", using a large star nozzle on to buttered baking trays. Bake at 350°F/180°C/gas mark 4 for 10–15 minutes until golden. Leave to cool on the tray.

Makes 24–36 depending on size of piping
***

SOFT BAKE MUESLI APPLE COOKIES

The soft bake result is achieved by omitting the sugar and using a sugar-free de-luxe muesli.

Dry muesli 8 oz (225 g)
Unrefined brown sugar (optional) 2 oz (50 g)
Wholemeal flour 4 oz (100 g)
Ground almonds 3 oz (75 g)
Large dessert apple, cored and grated 1
Butter 6 oz (175 g)
Honey 3 tbsp (45 ml)
Bicarbonate of soda ½ tsp (2.5 ml)

Combine the muesli, sugar (if used), flour, ground almonds and grated apple. Melt the butter and honey in a small saucepan. Remove from the heat and stir in the bicarbonate of soda. Mix well into the dry ingredients. Place generous spoonfuls of mixture on to buttered baking trays and flatten slightly.

Bake at 375°F/190°C/gas mark 5 for about 15–20 minutes or until golden. Cool on a wire tray.

Makes 16–20
***

HONEY FLORENTINES

Chewy and very special – serve them with coffee.

Butter 3 oz (75 g)
Honey 3 oz (75 g)
Walnuts, chopped 4 oz (100 g)
Flaked almonds 2 oz (50g)
Dried fruit, e.g. sultanas, pineapple or papaya,
finely diced 2 oz (50 g)
Wholemeal flour 1 oz (25 g)

TOPPING
Carob chips or carob bar, broken 4 oz (100 g)
Whipping cream 2 tbsp (30 ml)

Melt the butter and honey together in a saucepan over a gentle heat. Carefully stir in the remaining ingredients. Place large spoonfuls of the mixture well apart on baking trays covered with non-stick paper. Bake at 350°F/180°C/gas mark 4 for about 12 minutes or until golden. Cool on the tray.

When completely cold and set (you may wish to refrigerate them for a short time), make the topping. Melt the carob chips and cream together in a small bowl over a saucepan of simmering water. Coat the flat side of each Florentine with carob and mark into wavy lines using a fork. Allow to set.

Makes 10–12
***

POP CORN CHEWS

Children love these crunchy balls which can be made either with a sticky coating or more crispy, like a hard caramel.

Corn oil 1 tsp (5 ml)
Corn for popping 4 oz (100 g)
Salt, a pinch
Raisins 3 oz (75 g)
Hazelnuts, roasted and chopped 2 oz (50 g)
Barley malt syrup ¼ pt (150 ml)

Brush the bottom of a heavy-based large saucepan with the oil. Heat until fairly hot but not smoking and add the pop corn, shake the pan, then cover with the lid. Over a medium heat, the corn should start to pop after a minute or so. Shake occasionally to prevent burning. When the popping has stopped, tip the popcorn into a bowl. (It is very important to remove any corn that has not popped as this is difficult to eat and digest.) Add the salt, raisins and hazelnuts.

Heat the barley malt syrup until bubbling then pour over the popcorn, mixing to coat evenly. With wet hands, shape the popcorn mixture into balls, pressing them together firmly.

Either chill in the refrigerator to set the malt or place in the oven for 3–4 minutes at 350°F/180°C/gas mark 4 for a harder, crisper result.

Makes about 10

MAPLE SNAPS

These delicate biscuits harden very quickly, so it is essential to cook only two in each batch to allow time for shaping.

Butter 2 oz (50 g)
Unrefined brown sugar 2 oz (50 g)
Maple syrup 2 oz (50 g)
Wholemeal flour 2 oz (50 g)
Salt, a pinch
Ground ginger ½ tsp (2.5 ml)
Lemon juice or brandy ½ tsp (2.5 ml)
Double cream, whipped or Greek yoghourt
to fill

Line the baking trays with non-stick paper. Melt the butter, sugar and maple syrup over a low heat. Remove from the heat and stir in the flour, salt, ginger, lemon juice or brandy. Place teaspoons of the mixture on the prepared trays. Allow plenty of room for the mixture to spread. Bake at 350°F/180°C/gas mark 4 for about 8–10 minutes until the biscuits are golden, bubbly and lacy in texture.

Allow the biscuits to cool for about 1 minute, then loosen with a palette knife before rolling gently round the handles of wooden spoons. Allow to set, then remove the spoon handles. If the biscuits set before you have time to roll them, return them to the oven for a few seconds to soften.

Just before serving, fill the snaps with whipped cream or Greek yoghourt. Unfilled snaps will keep in an airtight container for up to 2 weeks.

Makes 20
*** without filling

FRUIT MINCE SLICE

Delicious lemon flavoured shortbread, sandwiched
with a sweet mincemeat filling makes the perfect
combination.

Wholemeal flour 9 oz (250 g)
Butter 6 oz (175 g)
Unrefined brown sugar 3 oz (75 g)
Lemon, finely grated rind of 1
Cranks fruit mincemeat 8 oz (225 g) (see p. 85)

Rub the butter into the flour until the mixture
resembles fine crumbs, then add the sugar and lemon
rind. Work together to form a firm dough, kneading
lightly. Roll out half the dough on a lightly floured
surface and press into a buttered 11×7 in (28×18 cm)
cake tin. Spread with the mincemeat. Roll out the
remaining shortbread and press lightly over the
mincemeat. Prick the surface with a fork. Bake at
325°F/160°C/gas mark 3 for about 45 minutes. Leave
in the tin to cool before cutting into slices.

Makes 12 slices
***

HONEY SHORTBREAD

The addition of honey gives a distinctive flavour to these traditional biscuits, so choose a fragrant blend.

Butter 4 oz (100 g)
Wholemeal flour 5 oz (150 g)
Brown rice flour 1 oz (25 g)
Honey 1 oz (25 g)

Rub the butter into the flour and rice flour until the mixture resembles fine crumbs. Add the honey and work together to form a dough. Knead lightly, then roll into a round. Press into a 7 in (18 cm) sandwich tin, neatening the edges and pricking the surface with a fork. Mark into 8 portions. Bake at 300°F/150°C/gas mark 2 for about 45 minutes. Cut into pieces while still warm, but leave in the tin to cool.

Alternatively, press the mixture into a shortbread mould and turn out on to a buttered baking tray for cooking.

Makes 8 pieces
***

CAROB NUTTY FLAPJACKS

Butter 5 oz (150 g)
Molasses 1½ oz (40 g)
Malt extract 1½ oz (40 g)
Honey ½ oz (15 g)
Hazelnuts, roasted and chopped 1 oz (25 g)
Rolled oats 8 oz (225 g)
Salt, a pinch
Orange-flavoured carob bar, chopped 2 oz (50 g)

Melt the butter, molasses, malt extract and honey
together over a gentle heat. Stir in the hazelnuts, oats
and salt. Allow to cool slightly, then mix in the
chopped carob bar. Press into a buttered and base-
lined shallow 7½ in (19 cm) square cake tin and bake
at 350°F/180°C/gas mark 4 for 20–25 minutes. Cut
into bars while still warm. Cool on a wire tray.

Makes 8 bars
***

NUT & RAISIN FLAPJACKS

Butter 3 oz (75 g)
Honey 1 tbsp (15 ml)
Molasses 1 tbsp (15 ml)
Vanilla essence ½ tsp (2.5 ml)
Unrefined brown sugar 2 oz (50 g)
Rolled oats 8 oz (225 g)
Raisins 2 oz (50 g)
Walnuts, chopped 2 oz (50 g)

Melt the butter, honey, molasses, vanilla essence and
sugar together in a saucepan. Stir in the oats, raisins

and chopped walnuts. Press into a buttered shallow 8 in (20 cm) square cake tin and bake at 350°F/ 180°C/gas mark 4 for about 20 minutes or until golden. Cut into bars in the tin while still warm, then leave until set.

Makes 8 bars
***

CELERY CHEESE SABLES

These very delicate biscuits literally melt in the mouth!

Wholemeal flour 4 oz (100 g)
Salt, a pinch
Butter 4 oz (100 g)
Cheddar cheese, grated 4 oz (100 g)
Free-range egg, separated 1
Celery seeds 1 tbsp (15 ml)
Paprika 1 tsp (5 ml)

Combine the flour and salt and rub in the butter. Stir in the grated cheese and bind together with the egg yolk. Knead lightly to form a dough. Roll out on a lightly-floured surface fairly thinly and cut into 2 in (5 cm) triangles.

Combine the celery seeds and paprika. Brush the biscuits with lightly-beaten egg white and sprinkle generously with the celery seed mixture.

Bake for about 10 minutes at 375°F/190°C/gas mark 5. Allow to cool a little before transferring to a wire tray.

Makes about 50
***

JAMMY DOUBLE DECKERS

Wholemeal flour 9 oz (250 g)
Ground almonds 1 oz (25 g)
Unrefined brown sugar 3 oz (75 g)
Butter 5 oz (150 g)
Free-range egg, beaten 1
Vanilla essence ½ tsp (2.5 ml)
Sugar-free raspberry or strawberry jam to fill

Place the flour, ground almonds and sugar in a bowl. Rub in the butter. Add the beaten egg and vanilla essence and mix to form a dough. Roll to about ¼ in (6 mm) thickness and stamp out rounds using a 2½ in (6.5 cm) fluted cutter. Cut a 1 in (2.5 cm) hole in the centre of half of the rounds.

Bake on buttered baking trays at 350°F/180°C/gas mark 4 for 10–15 minutes or until lightly golden. Cool on a wire tray.

When cold, spread the plain biscuits with jam and place the rings on top.

Makes 15
***

ORANGE CREAM KISSES

Unrefined brown sugar 4 oz (100 g)
Butter 4 oz (100 g)
Honey 2 tsp (10 ml)
Egg yolk 1
Orange, finely grated rind and juice of 1
Wholemeal flour 8 oz (225 g)
Baking powder 1 tsp (5 ml)

FILLING
Butter 3 oz (75 g)
Unrefined brown sugar 3 oz (75 g)

Cream the sugar, butter and honey until pale and fluffy. Beat in the egg yolk and the orange rind. Add the flour and baking powder and mix to a soft dough with the juice of half the orange.

Roll the dough into 24 small balls and place evenly spaced on buttered baking trays. Bake at 375°F/190°C/gas mark 5 for about 15 minutes or until golden. Cool on a wire tray.

For the filling, cream the butter and sugar until pale and thick. Beat in the remaining orange juice. Spread the filling over half of the biscuits and sandwich together.

Makes 12 biscuits
***

GINGERBREAD MEN

Try these for a children's tea party – the mixture can also be cut out in other shapes such as animals and flowers.

Wholemeal flour 1 lb (450 g)
Bicarbonate of soda 1 tbsp (15 ml)
Ground ginger 2 tsp (10 ml)
Ground cinnamon 1 tsp (5 ml)
Butter 4 oz (100 g)
Unrefined brown sugar 8 oz (225 g)
Molasses 4½ oz (115 g)
Honey 4½ oz (115 g)
Soya milk or milk if necessary
Pine kernels or currants to decorate

Place the flour, bicarbonate of soda, ginger and cinnamon in a bowl and mix well. Gently heat the butter, sugar, molasses and honey in a saucepan until just melted, then mix into the flour. If necessary add sufficient soya milk or milk to give a firm dough. Chill for 20–30 minutes.

Roll out to ¼ in (6 mm) thickness and stamp out gingerbread men using a special cutter. Place on baking trays which have been buttered or covered with non-stick paper and press pine kernels or currants in to make eyes, mouth and buttons. Bake at 325°F/160°C/gas mark 3 for about 15 minutes. Cool on a wire tray.

Makes about 25 five-inch (12.5 cm) biscuits
***

VALENTINE BISCUITS

These heart-shaped biscuits tell the whole story for
any romantic occasion!

Wholemeal flour 6 oz (175 g)
Medium oatmeal 1½ oz (40 g)
Baking powder 1 tsp (5 ml)
Salt ½ tsp (2.5 ml)
Butter 3 oz (75 g)
Unrefined brown sugar 2 oz (50 g)
Milk or soya milk to mix 3 tbsp (45 ml)

TOPPING
Carob chips or carob bar, broken 2 oz (50 g)
Whipping or single cream 2 tbsp (30 ml)

Place the flour, oatmeal, baking powder and salt in a
mixing bowl. Rub in the butter, then add the sugar.
Stir in the milk and mix to a firm dough. Roll out
fairly thinly on a lightly-floured surface and stamp out
biscuits using a heart-shaped cutter. Place on buttered
baking trays, prick the biscuits with a fork and bake at
350°F/180°C/gas mark 4 for about 20–25 minutes,
until golden. Cool on a wire tray.

For the topping, melt the carob chips and cream
together in a bowl over a saucepan of simmering
water. Dip either the bottom of each heart, or one side
into the carob. Leave to set on non-stick paper.

Store in an airtight tin.

Makes about 20 depending on cutter size
***

SESAME OATCAKES

A variation of traditional oatcakes, the sesame flavour
is enhanced by toasting the sesame seeds and using
sesame seed oil. Ideal for sweet or savoury snacks.

Fine oatmeal 10 oz (300 g)
Sesame seeds, toasted 1 oz (25 g)
Salt 1 tsp (5 ml)
Sesame seed oil 2 tbsp (30 ml)
Water ½ pt (300 ml)

Place the oatmeal, sesame seeds and salt in a bowl.
Bring the oil and water to the boil in a small saucepan
and pour into the dry ingredients, mixing thoroughly.
Allow to stand for a few minutes for the dough to
absorb the water, then knead until smooth.

Roll out on a surface lightly sprinkled with oatmeal
to just under ¼ in (6 mm) thickness. Stamp out
rounds using a 2¾ in (7 cm) plain cutter. Cook on a
hot griddle, turning half way through cooking, until
crisp and lightly coloured. Alternatively, bake in the
oven at 350°F/180°C/gas mark 4 for about 20–25
minutes. Cool on a wire tray.

Makes about 20
***

OATMEAL BISCUITS

Delicious, nutty and crumbly. Wonderful with cheese
or as sweet biscuits. Try them topped with melted
carob!

Wholemeal flour 8 oz (225 g)
Salt ½ tsp (2.5 ml)

Bicarbonate of soda ½ tsp (2.5 ml)
Butter 3 oz (75 g)
Nutter 3 oz (75 g)
Rolled oats 6 oz (175 g)
Coarse oatmeal 2 oz (50 g)
Unrefined brown sugar 2 oz (50 g)
Milk or soya milk 4 fl oz (100 ml)

Place the flour, salt and bicarbonate of soda in a bowl. Rub in the butter and nutter. Add the rolled oats, oatmeal and sugar and mix with the milk to make a firm dough. Roll out on a lightly-floured surface about ⅛ in (3 mm) thick. Stamp out 3 in (7.5 cm) rounds and bake on oiled baking trays at 400°F/200°C/gas mark 6 for about 15 minutes until lightly golden. Cool on a wire tray.

Makes about 27
***

GINGER SNAPS

Wholemeal flour 8 oz (225 g)
Salt, a pinch
Unrefined brown sugar 4 oz (100 g)
Butter 4 oz (100 g)
Maple syrup 4 fl oz (100 ml)
Ground ginger 1½ tsp (7.5 ml)
Bicarbonate of soda ¾ tsp (3.75 ml)

Combine the flour, salt and sugar in a mixing bowl. Melt the butter and maple syrup together over a gentle heat. Remove from the heat and add the ginger and bicarbonate of soda. Mix into the dry ingredients to form a soft dough. Roll into balls about the size of walnuts. Place well apart on oiled baking trays and flatten slightly. Bake at 375°F/190°C/gas mark 5 for about 15 minutes. Cool on a wire tray.

Makes 27–30 biscuits
***

PEPPERMINT CRISPS

These light, crisp biscuits are lovely for a special occasion as a contrast with ice creams, creamy desserts and fruits.

Egg white 1
Unrefined brown sugar 2 oz (50 g)
Peppermint essence ½ tsp (2.5 ml)
Butter 1 oz (25 g)
Wholemeal flour ½ oz (15 g)
Carob powder, sieved ½ oz (15 g)

Whisk the egg white until stiff. Whisk in the sugar a little at a time until smooth, then add the peppermint essence. Melt the butter and stir into the mixture, alternating with the flour and carob powder.

Place 2 teaspoonfuls (10 ml) of the mixture, well apart, on to oiled baking trays. Spread the mixture very thinly to about 4 in (10 cm) diameter. Bake at 375°F/190°C/gas mark 5 for about 5 minutes. Remove with a palette knife, and while still hot, curl over a lightly-greased rolling pin and leave to cool. Store in an airtight container.

Variations
Lemon Crisps
Replace the peppermint essence with the finely grated rind of 1 lemon. Use 1 oz (25 g) flour instead of ½ oz (15 g) flour and ½ oz (15 g) carob powder.

Orange Crisps
As Lemon Crisps but use orange rind.

Vanilla or Almond Crisps
Replace the peppermint essence with ½ tsp (2.5 ml) vanilla or almond essence. Use 1 oz (25 g) flour instead of ½ oz (15 g) flour and ½ oz carob powder.

Makes 14
***

SESAME SEED SQUARES

These golden chewy malted squares are lovely for
children and are quick and simple to make.

Malt extract 3 oz (75 g)
Sesame seeds, roasted 2 oz (50 g)
Jumbo oats 4 oz (100 g)
Sultanas 2 oz (50 g)
Sunflower oil 4 tbsp (60 ml)

Gently heat the malt extract until liquid. Mix into the
remaining ingredients and press into an oiled shallow
7½ in (19 cm) square tin. Bake at 350°F/180°C/gas
mark 4 for 20–30 minutes until golden. Cool in the tin,
cutting into squares while still warm.

Store in an airtight tin.

Variation
Use honey instead of malt extract for a lighter colour
and less chewy texture.

Makes 9 squares
***

CAROB CHIP & PECAN COOKIES

Butter 6 oz (175 g)
Self-raising wholemeal flour 8 oz (225 g)
Unrefined brown sugar 4 oz (100 g)
Salt, a pinch
Carob bar, broken 2.8 oz (80 g)
Pecan nuts, chopped 2 oz (50 g)
Free-range egg, beaten 1
Vanilla essence ½ tsp (2.5 ml)

Rub the butter into the flour. Add the sugar, salt, carob and pecan nuts. Mix to a soft dough with the egg and vanilla essence. With lightly-floured hands, roll the dough into 20 balls, about the size of large walnuts. Place well apart on oiled baking trays and press each to flatten slightly. Bake at 350°F/180°C/gas mark 4 for about 15 minutes or until golden brown. Cool on a wire tray.

Makes 20
***

BANANA & PEANUT COOKIES

These cookies are sweetened naturally with dates and banana. For those with a sweeter tooth, add 2 oz (50 g) sugar.

Butter 4 oz (100 g)
Banana, mashed 1
Lemon, finely grated rind of ½
Peanut butter 3 oz (75 g)

Free-range egg, beaten 1
Peanuts, roughly chopped 3 oz (75 g)
Dried dates, stoned and chopped 2 oz (50 g)
Wholemeal flour 3 oz (75 g)
Baking powder ½ tsp (2.5 ml)
Flaked wheat 5 oz (150 g)
Milk 4 tbsp (60 ml)

Cream the butter, banana, lemon rind and peanut butter until light and fluffy. Gradually beat in the egg, then stir in the remaining ingredients. Place spoonfuls of the mixture on to an oiled baking tray. Bake at 350°F/180°C/gas mark 4 for about 20–25 minutes until golden. Cool on a wire tray.

Makes 20
***

MILLET & ALMOND COOKIES

Oil 4 tbsp (60 ml)
Salt ¼ tsp (1.25 ml)
Free-range egg 1
Unrefined brown sugar 3 oz (75 g)
Almond essence 3–4 drops
Almonds, roughly chopped 4 oz (100 g)
Raisins 3 oz (75 g)
Millet flakes 4 oz (100 g)

Whisk the oil, salt, egg, sugar and almond essence together until thick and creamy. Stir in the remaining ingredients, then chill for 30 minutes. With wet hands, form the mixture into 10 balls and place on lightly-oiled baking trays. Flatten slightly.

Bake at 350°F/180°C/gas mark 4 for about 20–25 minutes or until golden. Cool on a wire tray.

Makes 10 cookies
***

NORMANDY GALETTE

PASTRY
Wholemeal flour 8 oz (225 g)
Butter 6 oz (175 g)
Unrefined brown sugar 2 oz (50 g)
Vanilla essence ½ tsp (2.5 ml)
Egg yolks 2

FILLING & TOPPING
Cooking apples, cored and chopped 2 lb (900 g)
Lemon, finely grated rind and juice of 1
Butter 1 oz (25 g)
Honey 2 tbsp (30 ml)
Ground cloves, a pinch
Calvados or brandy (optional) 2 tbsp (30 ml)
Raw sugar icing 1 quantity (see p. 86)
Carob powder 1 tsp (5 ml)

For the pastry, work all the ingredients together to make a firm dough. Divide into three and roll each into an 8 in (20 cm) round. Place on baking trays covered with non-stick paper and prick the surface. Bake at 375°F/190°C/gas mark 5 for about 10–15 minutes or until pale golden. Cool on a wire tray.

For the filling, simmer the apples gently to a pulp with the lemon rind and juice. Add the butter, honey, cloves and Calvados and blend in a food processor until smooth. Allow to cool, then use to sandwich the three pastry layers together. Coat the top of the galette with the raw sugar icing, reserving 2 tbsp (30 ml). Quickly colour the reserved icing with the carob powder, then place in a small greaseproof paper piping bag and use to pipe lines across the galette. "Feather" the icing by drawing the tip of a knife across the lines in alternate directions. Leave to set.

*** pastry rounds only

HAZELNUT APPLE SHORTCAKE

Butter 8 oz (225 g)
Unrefined brown sugar 2 oz (50 g)
Instant coffee 2 tsp (10 ml)
Boiling water 1 tbsp (15 ml)
Hazelnuts, roasted and ground 3 oz (75 g)
Wholemeal flour 10 oz (300 g)

Filling: *Dessert apples, cored and sliced 3*
Apricot jam 2 tbsp (30 ml)
Lemon, finely grated rind and juice of ½
Topping: *Carob chips or bar, broken 2 oz (50 g)*
Honey 2 tsp (10 ml)
Butter 1 oz (25 g)
Hazelnuts, roasted and coarsely chopped, to decorate

Cream the butter and sugar until pale and fluffy.
Dissolve the coffee in the boiling water, then mix into
the creamed mixture with the ground hazelnuts and
the flour to form a soft dough. Divide the dough in
half and roll each portion on a lightly-floured surface
into an 8½ in (22 cm) round. Cut out two 8½ in
(22 cm) circles of non-stick paper. Place the circles of
paper on baking trays and place the dough on top.
Crimp the edges to form neat rounds. Bake at 325°F/
160°C/gas mark 3 for about 40–45 minutes until crisp
and golden. Leave on the tray until cold.

For the filling, place all ingredients in a small
saucepan. Cover and simmer gently until the apples
are just soft but not mushy. Leave to go cold.

To assemble, place one shortcake carefully on a
serving plate. Cover with the apple mixture, then top
with the remaining shortcake.

For the topping, gently melt the carob, honey and
butter together, then pour over the cake. Decorate
with the hazelnuts.

*** shortcake rounds only

BLACKCURRANT CAROB CHOUX RING

An attractive centre piece, choux pastry always needs to be eaten the same day as it loses its crispness.

Choux pastry 1 quantity (see p. 91)

CAROB SAUCE
Carob chips or bar, broken 4 oz (100 g)
Honey 2 tsp (10 ml)
Butter 2 oz (50 g)

FILLING
Whipping cream ½ pt (300 ml)
Honey 2 tbsp (30 ml)
Blackcurrants, fresh or frozen 1 lb (450 g)

Shape the choux pastry into a 7 in (18 cm) ring on a piece of non-stick paper covering a baking tray. Bake at 425°F/220°C/gas mark 7 for about 30 minutes, until golden brown, well risen and firm. Split in half horizontally to allow the steam to escape. Allow to cool.

For the sauce, gently melt the carob, honey and butter together. Drizzle half over the top of the ring. Pour the remaining carob sauce into the base of the ring and allow to set.

For the filling, whip the cream into peaks then fold in the honey and blackcurrants. Fill the choux ring and replace the top.

COFFEE & CARAMEL
PROFITEROLES

Choux pastry 1 quantity (see p. 91)

Filling: *Instant coffee 1 tsp (5 ml)*
Boiling water 1 tsp (5 ml)
Quark 7 oz (200 g)
Egg white 1
Unrefined brown sugar 1 oz (25 g)

CARAMEL SAUCE
Unrefined brown sugar 4 oz (100 g)
Cold water 6 tbsp (90 ml)
Warm water 4 tbsp (60 ml)
Brandy or rum 2 tbsp (30 ml)

Using a ½ in (1.5 cm) plain nozzle, pipe about 20 choux pastry mounds on to buttered baking trays. Bake at 425°F/220°C/gas mark 7 for about 20– 25 minutes until well risen, crisp and golden. Make a small slit in each one to allow the steam to escape. Cool on a wire tray.

For the filling, dissolve the coffee in the hot water and add to the quark. Whisk the egg white until stiff, then whisk in the sugar until thick, smooth and glossy. Fold into the coffee quark.

For the sauce, place the sugar and the cold water in a saucepan and heat very gently. Shake the saucepan until the sugar dissolves but do not stir or the sugar will crystallize. Bring to the boil and cook steadily to a thick syrup, then continue boiling a little longer to a rich caramel. Remove from the heat and hold the pan over a bowl of lukewarm water so the base just touches the water. This will prevent further cooking. Carefully pour in the warm water and return to the heat to dissolve the caramel. Add the brandy and cool. Pipe the filling into the buns and pile them on to a serving plate. Pour the sauce over the profiteroles.

Makes about 20   77

RUM & RAISIN TOFU CAKE

This sugar- and dairy-free tofu cake consists of a crunchy base which contrasts well with the rum and raisin filling.

BASE
Margarine 4 oz (100 g)
Malt extract 1 oz (25 g)
Molasses 1 oz (25 g)
Rolled oats 6 oz (175 g)

FILLING
Raisins 6oz (175 g)
Rum 4 fl oz (100 ml)
Tofu 1 lb (450 g)
Tahini 2 tsp (10 ml)
Apple concentrate 4 fl oz (100 ml)
Orange, finely grated rind of ½
Orange, juice of 1
Agar flakes 1 tbsp (15 ml)

TOPPING
Water ¼ pt (150 ml)
Apple concentrate 1 tsp (5 ml)
Agar flakes 2 tsp (10 ml)
Rum 1 tbsp (15 ml)
Oranges 2

Soak the raisins overnight in 5 tbsp (75 ml) of the rum. Line an 8 in (20 cm) spring release tin with non-stick paper. Melt the margarine, malt extract and molasses together in a saucepan. Add the rolled oats, then press on to the base of the prepared tin. Bake for 15 minutes at 375°F/190°C/gas mark 5.

Blend the tofu, tahini, apple concentrate, orange rind and juice, agar flakes and the remaining rum in a food processor. Stir in the soaked raisins with their liquid. Pour on to the cooked biscuit base and return

to the oven at 350°F/180°C/gas mark 4 for about
40–45 minutes or until set. Allow to cool in the tin.

For the topping, place all the ingredients, except the
oranges, in a saucepan and bring to the boil. Simmer
for 5 minutes to dissolve the agar flakes. Peel and
thinly slice the oranges. Arrange on the surface of the
cake. Cool the topping and when it begins to set,
spoon carefully over the oranges. Chill in the
refrigerator until required.

BAKED CHEESECAKE PIE

This baked cheesecake is made with low fat cottage
cheese. For a richer cake use curd or cream cheese
and decorate the finished cake with fresh fruit and
cream.

Rich wholemeal shortcrust pastry 1 quantity (see p. 89)
Cottage cheese, sieved 8 oz (225 g)
Butter 1 oz (25 g)
Unrefined brown sugar 2 oz (50 g)
Lemon, finely grated rind of ½
Vanilla essence ½ tsp (2.5 ml)
Double cream 2 tbsp (30 ml)
Free-range eggs, separated 2
Sultanas 2 oz (50 g)

Line a deep-sided 8 in (20 cm) French fluted flan tin
with the pastry. Beat the cottage cheese, butter, sugar,
lemon rind, cream and egg yolks until smooth. Stir in
the sultanas. Whisk the egg whites until stiff, then fold
into the cheese mixture. Pour into the pastry case and
bake at 400°F/200°C/gas mark 6 for about 35 minutes
until risen, golden brown and set.

Allow to cool in the tin.

CAROB, ALMOND & PRUNE GÂTEAU

A rich carob gâteau, popular in Cranks Restaurants.

Butter 6 oz (175 g)
Unrefined brown sugar 6 oz (175 g)
Free-range eggs, separated 6
Almond essence ½ tsp (2.5 ml)
Vanilla essence ½ tsp (2.5 ml)
Self-raising wholemeal flour 2½ oz (65 g)
Carob powder, sieved 2 oz (50 g)
Ground almonds 3 oz (75 g)
Filling: Pitted prunes 8 oz (225 g)
Orange juice 8 fl oz (250 ml)
Decoration: Carob chips or bar, broken 1 oz (25 g)
Whipping or double cream ½ pt (300 ml)
Flaked almonds, toasted 2 oz (50 g)
Flaked carob to sprinkle (see p. 89)

Cream the butter and sugar until very pale and fluffy. Gradually beat in the egg yolks and the almond and vanilla essence. Combine the dry ingredients in a separate bowl and whisk the egg whites until stiff. Alternately, fold in the egg whites and the dry ingredients to the creamed mixture. Divide the mixture between two 8 in (20 cm) base lined sandwich tins. Bake at 350°F/180°C/gas mark 4 for about 30 minutes. Cool on a wire tray.

For the filling, simmer the prunes in the orange juice until soft. Purée to a smooth consistency in a food processor. When cool, use to sandwich the cake together.

For the decoration, gently melt the carob chips in a small saucepan with 3 tbsp (45 ml) of the cream to produce a smooth sauce. Leave to cool. Whip the remaining cream to a piping consistency then fold in the cool sauce. Spread the sides of the gâteau with a quarter of the cream, then press the toasted almonds on to the cream. Place on a serving dish. Cover the top of the cake with a layer of cream and, using a large star nozzle, pipe a border of cream. Fill the centre of the gâteau with flaked carob.

*** without decoration

COFFEE & WALNUT CREAM RING

This cake has a lovely light texture made moist with coffee and topped with a fluffy whipped cream. Ideal as a dessert.

Butter 6 oz (175 g)
Unrefined brown sugar 6 oz (175 g)
Free-range eggs, beaten 3
Self-raising wholemeal flour 6 oz (175 g)
Walnuts, chopped 3 oz (75 g)
Decaffeinated coffee, strong and freshly brewed
½ pt (300 ml)
Brandy or rum (optional) 2 tbsp (30 ml)
Whipped cream to decorate
Walnut halves 8

Cream the butter and sugar until pale, light and fluffy. Gradually beat in the eggs, then fold in the flour and walnuts. Turn into a well buttered 8 in (20 cm) Gugelhopf mould or ring mould and bake at 375°F/ 190°C/gas mark 5 for about 40 minutes or until well risen and springy to the touch. Cool on a wire tray. Return the cake to the clean mould, add the brandy to the coffee and spoon over the cake so that it soaks up all the coffee. Turn the ring on to a serving dish. Pipe swirls of cream on the top to decorate and finish with the walnut halves. Chill before serving.

*** without cream

HAZELNUT, COFFEE & RASPBERRY GÂTEAU

This Cranks recipe uses raspberries but other soft
fruits like blackberries or strawberries may be used in
this attractive summer gâteau.

Butter 6 oz (175 g)
Unrefined brown sugar 6 oz (175 g)
Free-range eggs, separated 6
Hazelnuts, toasted and finely ground 3 oz (75 g)
Self-raising wholemeal flour 2½ oz (65 g)

FILLING
Whipping or double cream ⅓ pt (200 ml)
Fresh raspberries 8 oz (225 g)
Hazelnuts, roasted and coarsely chopped 3 oz (75 g)

BUTTER CREAM ICING
Instant coffee 1 tsp (5 ml)
Water 1 tbsp (15 ml)
Unrefined brown sugar 2 oz (50 g)
Egg yolks 3
Butter, cubed 4 oz (100 g)

Cream the butter and sugar until very pale and fluffy.
Gradually beat in the egg yolks. Combine the ground
hazelnuts and flour. Whisk the egg whites in a
separate bowl until stiff, then alternately fold the dry
ingredients and the egg whites into the creamed
mixture. Divide the mixture between two 8 in (20 cm)
base-lined sandwich tins. Bake at 350°F/180°C/gas
mark 4 for about 25 minutes. Cool on a wire tray.

For the filling, whip the cream until it holds its
shape. Reserve 14 raspberries for decoration, then fold
the remainder into two-thirds of the cream. Use this to
fill the centre of the gâteau. Smooth the remaining
cream round the sides of the gâteau, then roll in the
toasted hazelnuts to coat evenly.

For the butter cream, dissolve the coffee in the water in a small saucepan. Add the sugar, then bring to the boil to dissolve. Remove from the heat, cool slightly, then whisk in the egg yolks one at a time. Finally, beat in the butter, a cube at a time. Blend thoroughly, then spread two-thirds over the top of the cake. Pipe rosettes of butter cream around the edge and decorate with the reserved fruit.

***

TRIPLE LAYER ORANGE GÂTEAU

A delicious gâteau but children may prefer it sandwiched with orange or carob butter cream and without the crystallized ginger.

Orange wholemeal whisked sponge mixture 1 quantity
(see p. 11)
Sugar-free apricot jam or marmalade 8 oz (225 g)
Double cream ½ pt (300 ml)
Crystallized ginger, chopped 1 oz (25 g)
Orange segments 12

Prepare the sponge mixture. Divide it between 3 sandwich tins. Bake for 15 minutes.

When cool, spread a layer of apricot jam or marmalade on the surface of each sponge layer.

Whip the cream until it holds its shape, then place one-third in a piping bag fitted with a large star nozzle. Chill until required. Fold the chopped ginger into the remaining cream and spread over the jam on two of the sponge layers.

Assemble the gâteau, finishing with the glazed layer. Decorate by piping the reserved cream around the top edge. Lay the orange segments across the cream.

*** without fresh orange

CHESTNUT CAROB GÂTEAU

Cranks used canned, unsweetened chestnut purée.
You could prepare your own purée from fresh or
soaked dried chestnuts.

Free-range eggs 6
Unrefined brown sugar 6 oz (175 g)
Vanilla essence ½ tsp (2.5 ml)
Chestnut purée, beaten smooth 12 oz (350 g)
Wholemeal flour 3 oz (75 g)
Butter, melted 3 oz (75 g)

FILLING
Whipping cream ¼ pt (150 ml)
Carob chips or bar, broken 2 oz (50 g)
Orange marmalade 6 tbsp (90 ml)

TOPPING
Carob chips or bar, broken 6 oz (175 g)
Whipping cream 4 tbsp (60 ml)
Butter 2 oz (50 g)
Egg yolks 2

Whisk the eggs and sugar over a saucepan of
simmering water until thick and pale. The whisk
should leave a thick trail in the mixture. Add the
vanilla essence and the chestnut purée. Gently fold in
the flour and finally the butter. Divide between three
buttered and base-lined 8 in (20 cm) sandwich tins
and bake at 375°F/190°C/gas mark 5 for about 30
minutes. Cool on a wire tray.

For the filling, whip the cream until stiff. Divide into
two. Melt the carob over a pan of simmering water,
cool and fold into half of the cream. When the cakes
are cool, spread one with half the marmalade, then
cover with the carob cream. Place the second cake on
top, spread with the remaining marmalade and the
plain cream. Top with the third sponge.

For the topping, place the carob, cream and butter in a bowl and melt over a saucepan of simmering water. Remove from the heat, cool slightly then beat in the egg yolks. As the topping cools, it will become thicker. When this begins to happen, pour half over the top of the gâteau and smooth to make a glossy finish. Beat the remaining icing and when it is quite cold, using a large nozzle, pipe rosettes on top of the gâteau to decorate.

***

CRANKS FRUIT MINCEMEAT

Nutter 1 oz (25 g)
Raisins 3 oz (75 g)
Sultanas 3 oz (75 g)
Currants 3 oz (75 g)
Unrefined brown sugar 2 oz (50 g)
Ground cinnamon ¼ tsp (1.25 ml)
Ground nutmeg ¼ tsp (1.25 ml)
Ground mixed spice ¼ tsp (1.25 ml)
Orange, grated rind and juice of ½
Lemon, grated rind and juice of ½
Cooking apple, cored and finely chopped 4 oz (100 g)
Flaked almonds ½ oz (15 g)
Brandy 1–2 tbsp (15–30 ml)

Mix all the ingredients together except for the cooking apples, flaked almonds and brandy and leave covered overnight.

Mix in the apple, then transfer to a deep ovenproof dish. Cover with a lid or foil and bake at 250°F/120°C/gas mark ½ for 1 hour. Stir well half-way through the cooking time. Leave to cool before adding the almonds and the brandy. Store in the refrigerator.

CRANKS RAW SUGAR LEMON CURD

Lemons, finely grated rind and juice of 2
Unrefined light brown sugar 8 oz (225 g)
Butter, cubed 4 oz (100 g)
Free-range eggs, beaten 3

Place all the ingredients in the top of a double boiler or in a bowl over a pan of simmering water. Heat gently, stirring until the curd thickens and will coat the back of a wooden spoon.

Pour into clean, dry, warm jars and cover immediately.

Variation
For a change, substitute oranges for lemons and add the juice of 1 lemon to make orange curd. Store in the refrigerator.

Makes about 1 lb (450 g)

RAW SUGAR ICING

Unrefined brown sugar 4 oz (100 g)
Lemon or orange juice to mix
Vanilla or almond essence, a few drops

Mill the sugar very finely in a coffee grinder. Add sufficient lemon or orange juice and essence to give a coating consistency and beat until smooth.

Variation
Coffee or Carob Icing
Replace the lemon juice with 1 tsp (5 ml) instant coffee or carob powder dissolved in sufficient boiling water to give a coating consistency.

BUTTER CREAM

Butter 4 oz (100 g)
Unrefined brown sugar 8 oz (225 g)
Milk and/or flavouring (see below) 3 tbsp (45 ml)

Cream the butter and sugar until very pale and fluffy.
Beat in the milk and/or flavouring.

Sufficient to fill and cover an 8 in (20 cm) cake.

Variations
Vanilla
Beat in ½ tsp (2.5 ml) vanilla essence with the milk.

Coffee
Replace 1 tbsp (15 ml) milk with 2 tsp (10 ml) instant
coffee, dissolved in 1 tbsp (15 ml) hot water or milk.
Cool before adding.

Carob
Replace 2 tbsp (30 ml) milk with 2 tbsp (30 ml) carob
powder, blended with 2 tbsp (30 ml) hot water or
milk. Cool before adding.

Orange or Lemon
Replace the milk with the finely grated rind of 1
orange or lemon and 3 tbsp (45 ml) juice.

ALMOND PASTE

Ground almonds 6 oz (175 g)
Unrefined brown sugar 4 oz (100 g)
Lemon juice 1 tsp (5 ml)
Sherry or brandy 2 tsp (10 ml)
Vanilla essence ½ tsp (2.5 ml)
Almond essence ¼ tsp (1.25 ml)
Free-range egg, beaten 1 tbsp (15 ml)

Mix the ground almonds and the sugar in a bowl, breaking down any small lumps. Combine all the remaining ingredients, then add to the almonds and work together to form a smooth paste.

Makes about 11 oz (325 g)

APRICOT MARZIPAN

Dried apricots, chopped 3 oz (75 g)
Sultanas 1 oz (25 g)
Lemon, juice of ½
Apple concentrate 2 tbsp (30 ml)
Sherry or brandy 2 tsp (10 ml)
Water 2 tbsp (30 ml)
Ground almonds 1 lb (450g)
Soya flour 2 oz (50 g)
Almond essence ½ tsp (2.5 ml)

Soak the apricots and sultanas overnight in the lemon juice, apple concentrate and sherry.

Place the soaked ingredients in a food processor and blend with the water to a smooth purée. Add the remaining ingredients and process well. Press together to form a smooth paste.

DECORATIONS

FLAKED CAROB
To make these delicate carob flakes, melt carob chips or broken carob bar in a bowl over a pan of simmering water. Do not allow it to get too hot. Pour on to a cold surface, such as marble or stainless steel, and allow to set. Using a large knife, shave flakes from the surface of the carob.

CAROB LEAVES
Using a fine, clean artist's paintbrush, coat the underside of small, fresh rose leaves with melted carob. Leave to set, carob-side up and then carefully peel away the leaf.

CAROB CURLS
Leave a carob bar at room temperature, then simply peel the carob curls from the bar with a potato peeler.

RICH WHOLEMEAL SHORTCRUST PASTRY

Butter 3 oz (75 g)
Wholemeal flour 4½ oz (115 g)
Unrefined brown sugar 1 oz (25 g)
Iced water 1 tbsp (15 ml)

Rub the butter into the flour until the mixture resembles fine crumbs. Stir in the brown sugar and mix to a firm dough with the water.

CRANKS PUFF PASTRY

This quantity may be cut into convenient sized pieces and frozen.

Puff pastry can be made successfully using 100 per cent wholemeal flour; however, the lighter the flour, the more it will puff up. Some of the bran may be sifted and kept for use in other recipes, such as Bran Biscuits.

Wholemeal flour 1 lb (450 g)
Salt 2 tsp (10 ml)
Butter 1 lb (450 g)
Cold water ½ pt (300 ml)
Lemon juice 1 tsp (5 ml)

Sieve the flour, if wished, into a mixing bowl and add the salt. Rub in 4 oz (100 g) of the butter. Add the cold water and lemon juice and mix to a firm pliable dough. Transfer to a lightly-floured surface and knead lightly until smooth.

Roll out to a rectangle approximately 15×10 in (38×25 cm). Work the remaining butter into an oblong shape between plastic sheets. It should be workable but not soft and oily, so chill in the refrigerator if necessary.

Place the butter centrally on the pastry and fold over the side flaps and then the top and bottom to cover completely the butter and form a neat parcel. Place seam side down.

Using firm but gentle pressure, press ridges down the length of the block with a rolling pin before carefully rolling once more into the large rectangle. Take care not to push the butter through. Mark the rectangle into three and fold the top third down over the centre third; fold the bottom third up over the other two thirds. Press the edges together at the sides, using the rolling pin. Place in a floured plastic bag and chill for ½ hour.

Place the folded pastry on a lightly-floured surface and turn through 90°. Repeat the rolling, folding and turning three more times, chilling for 30 minutes between the second and third rolling and before using as required in the recipe.

Makes approximately 2½ lb (1.2 kg)

CHOUX PASTRY

Recipes made with this pastry should always be
eaten the same day.

Butter 2 oz (50 g)
Water ¼ pt (150 ml)
Wholemeal flour 3 oz (75 g)
Free-range eggs, beaten 2

Place the butter and water in a saucepan and bring to the boil. Immediately tip in the flour, beating with a wooden spoon to form a smooth, shiny ball. Remove from the heat and allow to cool slightly. Gradually beat in the eggs to form a smooth paste.

WHOLEMEAL PASTRY CHART
easy guide to quantities

100% wholemeal flour	baking powder	½ butter ½ Nutter	water (approx)
4 oz (100 g)	1 tsp (5 ml)	2 oz (50 g)	4 tsp (20 ml)
5 oz (150 g)	1½ tsp (7.5 ml)	2½ oz (75 g)	2 tbsp (30 ml)
6 oz (175 g)	1½ tsp (7.5 ml)	3 oz (85 g)	2 tbsp (30 ml)
7 oz (200 g)	2 tsp (10 ml)	3½ oz (100 g)	3 tbsp (45 ml)
9 oz (250 g)	2½ tsp (12.5 ml)	4½ oz (125 g)	4 tbsp (60 ml)
10 oz (300 g)	3 tsp (15 ml)	5 oz (150 g)	4 tbsp (60 ml)
12 oz (350 g)	3 tsp (15 ml)	6 oz (175 g)	5 tbsp (75 ml)
14 oz (400 g)	4 tsp (20 ml)	7 oz (200 g)	5 tbsp (75 ml)

Place the flour and baking powder in a bowl. Rub in the fat until the mixture resembles fine crumbs. Add sufficient warm water to give a soft but manageable dough. Cover with cling film and leave at room temperature until ready to use.

US EQUIVALENTS

An American pint measures 16 fl oz (500 ml) and there are 2 cups (8 fl oz (250 ml) each) to the pint. The British pint is 20 fl oz (600 ml).

British Standard measuring spoons are:
1 teaspoon = 5 ml
1 tablespoon = 15 ml
Hence there are 3 teaspoons to one tablespoon.
An American tablespoon is 4 teaspoons (20 ml)

There is no easy guide for translating recipes from English to American but here are a few standard amounts.
1 cup butter = 8 oz (225 g)
1 cup sugar = 7 oz (200 g)
1 cup flour = 5 oz (150 g)

INDEX